EVERYWHERE FOR WALES

EVERYWHERE
FOR WALES

Phil Bennett
and Martyn Williams

Stanley Paul
London Melbourne Sydney Auckland Johannesburg

Stanley Paul & Co. Ltd

An imprint of the Hutchinson Publishing Group

17–21 Conway Street, London W1P 5HL

Hutchinson Group (Australia) Pty Ltd
30–32 Cremorne Street, Richmond South, Victoria 3121
PO Box 151, Broadway, New South Wales 2007

Hutchinson Group (NZ) Ltd
32–34 View Road, PO Box 40-086, Glenfield, Auckland 10

Hutchinson Group (SA) Pty Ltd
PO Box 337, Bergvlei 2012, South Africa

First published 1981
Reprinted October 1981

© Phil Bennett 1981

Set in Baskerville by
Computape (Pickering) Ltd, Pickering, North Yorkshire

Printed in Great Britain by The Anchor Press Ltd
and bound by Wm Brendon and Son Ltd
both of Tiptree, Essex

British Library Cataloguing in Publication Data

ISBN 0 09 146310 6

Contents

	Acknowledgements	6
1	Llanelli 9 Seland Newydd 3	7
2	Felinfoel	12
3	Llanelli	29
4	Wales – 'Follow me quietly'	45
5	Ups and Downs	69
6	South Africa	83
7	Touring is Fun?	97
8	All Blacks '77	112
9	My Kind of Guy	131
10	Paying My Round	146
11	'Who Are You Playing On Saturday?'	159
12	A Fitting End	173

Acknowledgements

Copyright photographs are acknowledged as follows:
Agence Presse Sports; Colorsport; Terry Downey;
Adrian Murrell; John Townsend; *Western Mail*; D. Peel.

1

Llanelli 9 Seland Newydd 3

As soon as I'd got out of bed I could sense the tension. I popped down to the local shop to buy a newspaper and there were people wandering about at ten a.m. dressed in red and white scarves and caps. Familiar faces would nod politely, but were somehow too shy to say anything, just in case the 'boy' would be upset by an untimely remark. A few passed in their cars, but today there were none of the customary raps on the horn. It was a strange sensation, but I gave it little thought at the time, since I had to be at the team hotel in under an hour.

The All Blacks had looked impressive in their first tour match against the Western Counties, but the Llanelli boys had returned from the tourists' match at Gloucester with determined grins on their faces. 'We can beat them,' they whispered. I nodded approvingly, though at the time I didn't believe a word of it.

On the way to the Ashburnham Hotel, I drove through the town. Llanelli had been attacked by a red virus. The streets were lined with old and young Scarlet loyalists, mothers accompanying eleven-year-olds with flags, leeks, rosettes and anything else that had a blotch of red on it . . . the whole place had surrendered willingly to Llanelli RFC. There were notices on shop windows announcing early closure, I could see friends on street corners who should have been at work. It did the trick, I started to get nervous. Nevertheless I was in a far healthier state than the rest of the team.

One look at them after I entered the hotel foyer said it

all. They hardly resembled a collection of hardy individuals who were about to do battle with the All Blacks. Tense, ashen-faced, irritable ... they looked really terrible! The comics of the side – 'Chico' Hopkins, Tommy David and Roy Thomas – were mute, a few looked at the newspapers but couldn't read, and then Carwyn James the coach, sensitive to the situation as ever, told us all to get out of the building and go for a walk.

The months of preparation had had all the trappings of a military operation. I had met Tommy David on a Crawshay tour in the West Country and he'd confided that he wasn't enjoying his rugby with Pontypridd. He watched Llanelli play the Barbarians and needed no encouragement after that to join forces with the Scarlets.

'Chico' Hopkins had also been restless at Maesteg, and he too had decided that his future belonged at Stradey Park. The two recruits no doubt strengthened our playing ability, but I did feel sorry for the established players, who because of the new arrivals had to settle for second best. During the week before the All Blacks match, in between the exhausting training sessions, Carwyn had invited me, the Llanelli skipper Delme Thomas, and the assistant coach Normal Gale out for a meal. He'd picked a restaurant in the wilds of Wales somewhere near Salem, Llandeilo. How we ever found the place and got back, I'll never know. But that was James ... he'd picked a place where nothing would distract us. We talked about tactics. The plan was quite simple – we would have to tackle everything in sight, make no mistakes, get down to the All Blacks line and then probe their defences.

The team returned from its walk. The breath of fresh air had done us a power of good. A bit of colour had returned to our cheeks and some players were even prepared to talk. We were called into a private room. The first to speak was the Welsh Rugby Union coaching adviser Ray Williams, who stressed the need for us to reach our potential. Carwyn was next, analytical as ever – lyrical – he'd nurtured most of us since we'd joined the

8

club, he knew our weaknesses and our strengths. He also had something to prove. He and the Lions had been successful in New Zealand in 1971, but this, a year later, was different, this was the home team – Llanelli. A win today would not only put Llanelli on the rugby map but it would prove beyond doubt that he was the world's leading coach. He didn't say that, but we all knew what the game meant to him. Norman Gale his assistant, fists clenched and nervous eyes, got up to speak. His speech, delivered in good Anglo-Saxon expletives, was to the point. By this time the pale looks had returned, the tension was unbearable. Delme, our captain, said a few words, but was keeping his final oration for the changing room. A police escort arrived to take us to Stradey.

Somehow the bus got through the thousands of staring faces. I remember thinking at the time, What happens if we lose? What will these people think of us then? Will they still look up to us as they're doing now? What am I going to tell them at work tomorrow if we're thrashed? Damn these All Blacks!

The skipper's phrases had been well worked out. 'I don't care what any of you have achieved . . . I am willing to give up all my caps, the Lions tours, anything, for this one today . . . this is your club, it's my club . . . those people out there who've been at the ground since dawn . . . it's their club too. Your wives are up in the stand, they're here to support you; there are hundreds of kids in Llanelli this afternoon who won't get into the ground, they'll all be listening on radios at home or watching the match on the television. The whole town will want to know how the Scarlets are getting on against New Zealand. Those people who are here, and those that would like to be here but can't get in. It is their club too.' Delme was standing in the middle of the changing room. His sleeves were rolled up. He waited so that he had everybody's attention. Delme, who worked on the top of telegraph poles and had a fascination for 'budgies', was about to put the fear of God into anyone who wouldn't follow him to the end.

'I'll give anything for a win – caps, tours, dinners, awards, anything. This is our day, if we fail then it's our fault. We are playing for Llanelli – not Wales or the British Lions – for Llanelli, your club, my club, those people out there . . . that is who you are playing for, and if you can look me in the eye at the end of the afternoon then you'll have given me a hundred per cent.'

He went around the room pointing his finger at each player, and asked every one of them in turn if they were going to support him.

'Andy? . . . Budgie? . . . Shanto? . . . Barry? Are you with me boys?' He stared each one in the eye. He was willing to sacrifice everything for the next eighty minutes, he'd said so. I fought back the tears, gritted my teeth and clenched my fists. In the end my resistance gave way, and I couldn't hold back the tears. The speech had got through to all of us. He'd timed it to perfection.

'OK, let's go,' and there were fifteen of us fighting to get through the door and out onto the field.

We played like a team possessed. Gareth Jenkins carried on with two cut eyes. Tony Croker took care of Keith Murdoch in the front, Derek Quinnell and Barry Llewelyn rammed their bodies against the All Black wall time after time, and Delme towered above the line-outs. Roy Bergiers got the try, Andy Hill kicked the goals and Llanelli won by 9 points to 3. The last ten minutes were the longest I've spent in rugby football.

When the whistle went for full time, the scenes were incredible. There was an element of hysteria in the changing room, as crying supporters asked for the laces from players' boots, others asked for socks and some of the old warriors came in and just smiled. I have never seen anything like it, and never will.

The pubs on the homeward roads from Stradey had run dry before we had changed. A man walked up to me and said that his wife had given birth to a boy that afternoon and he was now quite happy to go over to the hospital and see if mother and son were all right. He named the boy with the Christian names of the Llanelli team! A few supporters remained on the terraces, staring at the grass and savouring every memory of the afternoon's battle. Llanelli had beaten the All Blacks!

Though I went to work the next morning, the celebration party lasted a week – and on the Saturday we lost to Richmond!

2

Felinfoel

Felinfoel has never held any attraction for the tourist. It's an odd collection of industrial cottages, terraced streets and council houses, built on either side of the main Carmarthen – Llanelli road. Apart from the brewery building in the middle of the village, there is little to distract the motorist except the 30 m.p.h. speed limit. Like so many of the small towns and hamlets in that part of the world, Felinfoel is a monument to the busy age of the industrial revolution. The coalfields of the Gwendraeth and the furnaces of Llanelli brought prosperity to the area, and no one cared for environmental planning in those days. Yet I would change none of it, the years of familiarity with the streets and their people have welded an inseparable bond between me and them. Whether sitting in a hotel room in Christchurch, Cape Town, or Edinburgh, invariably my thoughts turn towards home, Felinfoel, an 'ugly, lovely town', if I may be so bold as to borrow a description from another Welshman. I could never live anywhere else, and I suspect that many would say that homesickness eventually led to my downfall as a Lions captain. They could be right!

We lived at 18 Heol Daniel, a council house with one of those warm open-hearth fireplaces. My father worked in the local steelworks, the 'Klondyke' as we used to call the place, since you didn't know whether you were working there from one week to the next. It was strenuous and demanding labour, ten hours a day in difficult conditions, but there were few alternatives. Indeed, it was Hobson's choice. You could either opt for work underground in the Gwendraeth valley mines or face the heat of the Llanelli furnaces. I remember the miners with their sandwich boxes in tow leaving on the early buses for Tumble and Cefneithin, but most of the village men opted for the economic uncertainty of the 'Klondyke'. Still, there was that great affinity between the colliers and the furnace workers, a bond that brought great unity to the village life. The hazards and physical strain of both jobs were well matched. So my father went to the steelworks where the men sacrificed themselves to the furnaces during the day, then regained the liquid lost from their bodies on the way home! At times, he would work through the night and arrive home at six in the morning. I remember the delight of hearing the hobnail boots coming down the path, around the back of the house, while we got up to enjoy a boiled egg with him.

One day though, the footsteps stopped at the front gate, and immediately I knew something was wrong. He eventually came through the door, but there was a wretched, tearful look on on his face. One of his mates had been knocked over by a big magnet at the works and had fallen into one of the molten pits. Emlyn Baddams had been a close friend, and another of the men, Ossie Williams, a huge man and a fiery forward for Llanelli, had to be restrained from jumping into the boiling metal to try and save his mate. My father had watched it all; they had seen a man being boiled alive, and the stench was to stay with my father for months afterwards.

The works provided the family with a wage. Meanwhile, though, the demands of a growing schoolboy made it necessary for my mother as well to go out and work, at the local car-pressing plant. My parents had both been married before but, by that time, three of my step-brothers and a step-sister had long gone from home. Oliver, another step-brother and the closest to me, remained. So that just left the four of us. It was a comfortable home, made happy because of my parents' devotion to each other. All through those years, even when my father had to give up work because of an industrial accident, there were never any complaints from my mother. Despite the fact that we had few luxuries, both made a conscious effort to see that I didn't go without. It may be unfashionable these days to take pride in one's parents, but I have nothing but admiration for the way I was brought up. They were carefree days, hours spent from dawn until dusk down on Felinfoel Park, listening to my father recite amazing tales of his pride and joy – Llanelli RFC.

I'd been born weak, rushed to hospital where I'm told that I nearly died because of a cervitus gland. 'Puny and fragile', is how the family recall the appearance of the newcomer. And many years later, Brian Thomas, the rugged captain of Neath, once said to a referee when we were about to toss up before a game, 'What's this rag doll? Send out a man to toss up!' The early years of my life were something of a worry for my parents. If there was a bug about, as sure as daylight 18 Heol Daniel would become a casualty ward. The doctor who looked after me during those years, when my parents beat a worn track with Bennett junior in tow to the local hospital, delivered my father a crushing blow during one of those visits. 'I'm sorry Mr Bennett, but this one will never have the physique to play rugby, and he may take a lot of looking after.'

It took only a few years for me to disprove the good doctor's prediction. Hours upon hours were spent on the playing field of Felinfoel. The sound of feet outside the door accompanied by a bouncing ball signalled the clarion call for all able-bodied tots – me included – to the park. The matches were endless: Wales against England, Llanelli against Swansea; I was John Charles towering up to crosses, three feet six in my stockinged feet! Dusk or a burst bladder were the only permitted excuses to bring to an end the international warfare. The only trouble with the park was that everybody else wanted a game, and it is only on the rare occasion that one touches the ball in a twenty-five-a-side battle. Mud-splattered and exhausted I would arrive home for a wash in the communal tub in front of the fire. My mother would frown at the amount of dirt that a *'tamaid bach'* (small one) could gather in one afternoon on his clothes. My father would smile and thank the Lord that doctors were fallible.

Ysgol-y-Babanod, the local infants' school, was a mere extension of the local playing fields. Little knowledge was acquired, apart from how to dodge past twenty boys on a concrete surface. The facilities were nil, the school playing-yard had to suffice as soccer, rugby and cricket stadia. The 'turf' taught me how to keep out of harm's way, since the alternatives of cut knees and grazed elbows were far too painful to contemplate. The next school, the Felinfoel County Primary, had a teacher called John Williams. He wasn't a PE teacher as such, just one of those people you find in small schools, dedicated to their pupils and their welfare. His forte was cricket, and since he was an exceptionally large man, or so it seemed to an eight-year-old, he would sling down cricket balls at his quivering batsmen with frightening speed. To us he was Wes Hall and Charlie Griffith combined, and to score a four against the wall of his 90 m.p.h. 'quickies' was a feat to savour. Most of the time though, he forced us to use defensive qualities.

Up until this time my father had merely taken a passing interest in my unremarkable progress; throughout the years of youth and senior rugby he has never interfered at all, leaving decisions and problems for me to sort out. However on one day, I was summoned to the headmaster's study.

A few of my friends as usual had been playing with a ball in the yard and were late in reacting to the bell summoning us back to the scholarly task of mastering the nine-times table. The ball was still being flicked around as we begrudgingly shuffled to the classroom. The ball went astray and a window was smashed. We were hauled before the headmaster, who wasn't known for his tolerance of such misdemeanours, and he gave the lot of us

15

a right old caning.

There was little I could do to hide the discomfort of the pain, but somehow I kept the punishment a secret from my parents. Behind my closed bedroom door, I even managed to complete a hundred lines that the headmaster had ordered the guilty to write. However, there was a Judas afoot.

'Do you know that your Philip was caned this afternoon in school, Mr Bennett?' The girl next door took great delight in my misery and told my astonished father the whole truth; no details were spared. He lost no time in summoning me before the fire to expose the damaged part. 'We'll see about that headmaster of yours tomorrow,' was all he muttered. To be summoned on successive days to the head's office was a frightening prospect, but when I turned the corner, the scene was far more terrifying than anything that I had anticipated.

There were four men in the corridor. My father, once he saw me, asked, 'Is this the man who put that stick over your backside?' The head master, his shirt and tie covering his chin, was being held up against the wall by Des 'Ginger' one of the largest men in Felinfoel. In case the assailants needed extra encouragement, my stepbrother Oliver also had his sleeves rolled up. The three had obviously spent some time contemplating this vengeful act in the 'Union' and Des, strengthened by the hop and motivated by a sense of justice, was ready to be judge and jury. 'Shall I let 'im 'av one now?' he asked. I pleaded with my father to let the headmaster go. The big man we all feared had been turned into a quivering apology, quite unable to comprehend what was happening. The smell on the breath of Des 'Ginger' had convinced him that the big brute in front of him would have no hesitation in unleashing a mighty blow to his chin.

My continual pleading for truce eventually met with favour and the headmaster was left to fall on the floor, graciously thanking me for my better sense. The musketeers left the school to tell the 'Union' regulars that they'd sorted 'that bugger' out. In fact, they had, since he left me well alone after that episode.

In a way my mother was far more protective, but would hardly have contemplated physical retribution against the local headmaster. After a full day's work at the factory she had to face another hard shift at home. Clothes had to be washed, socks darned and everything in the house dusted. The small oven over the fire would turn out punctual meals, though she would despair at my insistence on chips with everything. Welsh swearwords delivered in hushed tones signified displeasure of some sort, but there were never any complaints. When I eventually achieved an age old enough to go on school-boy trips abroad or to England, she would make sure that Mrs Bennett's boy was as smartly dressed as any of the others. You could call it pride, but I was never to go without anything. They realised very quickly that I would never achieve any scholastic distinction and so Christmas presents would invariably consist of soccer annuals or books written by sportsmen. But despite their efforts to be discreet Father Christmases, the burrowing little mischief had normally found the hiding place and had read every single word by Christmas morning.

I do remember disappointing my mother on one occasion. A stack of bibles at home will testify to my good attendance at Sunday school, but I recall my first visit with rare clarity. I was to be accompanied to this new adventure by two girls next door. Dressed to the 'nines', I must have looked the picture of innocence walking between my two keepers hand in hand towards the local chapel. I had no idea of what to except and nobody had bothered to tell me, but since most of the other children seemed to disappear from the park on a Sunday after-noon, the Sunday school had a certain magnetism.

As with all Welsh chapel events, the Sunday school order of proceedings had a certain rigidity about it: the hymn, the prayer, the class, then the gathering of the whole congregation for the announcements, and the children's verses. No one had bothered to forewarn me about the verses, where the younger element were expected to recite a verse or two from the Bible. The 'swots' of course would in grand Eisteddfodic manner, to the nodding approval of the elders, recite large chunks or even chapters of the Scriptures. But no one had told me of this particular requirement. Lining up with all the other children I scoured my brain for any verse that I had been taught. It was a bit much to ask anyone on his very first day to come up to scratch, but suddenly they were about to ask me for my inaugural contribution. To this day I don't remember who taught me this poetic gem, but out it came:

> 'Butcher, Butcher, kill a calf,
> Hang him up, and smack his arse!'

My two escorts cried all the way home, and there was more than a tear in my mother's eyes when told about my little rendering. I attended Sunday school until I was fourteen, when one day a brief detour on the way home to the muddy park and a severe spanking for spoiling my 'Sunday best' convinced me that life was far less hazardous without chapel. A decision that I've often regretted.

The other school, Coleshill Secondary Modern, was a different kettle of fish altogether.

Here there were organized games against neighbouring schools. These were new and exciting challenges that were awaited with great expectation and more than a little impatience. Even the limited practice sessions with the open-air park-bench changing rooms became tolerable. There were even corner flags on the odd occasion. Coleshill represented all that I'd ever wanted.

Our facilities, compared with the *crach* (posh) school in town, Llanelli Grammar School, were extremely poor and so it gave the boys from Coleshill enormous pleasure to beat the town school at anything. One master at the school was to have an enormous influence on my early days. Mervyn Bowen was not so much a rugby master or coach, as a philosopher. He had definite ideas on how one should play rugby. At first he played me in every position behind the scrum and I doubt that even Mr Bowen foresaw that I would eventually fill nearly all those positions in a senior Welsh jersey. Whatever the intention, it gave me the opportunity of learning the tasks of a wing, centre *or* scrum-half. But the master was to pass on a far more valuable lesson. We were playing Llanelli Grammar School, and Coleshill had managed to edge their way into a 6 point to nil lead. Victories against our rivals were all too infrequent and I remember deciding on a 'hug the touchline and kick everything in sight' tactic. The lead was preserved until the final whistle and we wallowed in the pride of sticking one on those grammar school boys. The next morning in school, Mr Bowen called me over and I fully expected to receive all the laurels for my part in the dramatic victory.

'You had a bad game yesterday, Phil, you forgot one essential factor. There were fourteen other boys on that field who wanted a game, and did you stop to think what the winger felt, when you were kicking the ball all over the place? There's more to the game than just winning!' I was speechless, and my disappointment was only deepened by gradually realizing that the master was right. It's a lesson that, I sometimes think, I and others tended to forget in the Welsh team, years later.

Llanelli has provided and always will provide a bottomless well of schoolboy talent, mainly because of the time devoted to the game by schoolmasters and well-meaning officials throughout the area. I find it quite remarkable that the standard remains so consistently high. Even in my age group the local schoolboys' team included Terry Price, Roy Mathias, Keith Hughes, Stuart Gallacher, and Kelvin Coslett in their ranks, all destined to become senior Welsh internationals. Another member and a great friend of mine, Brian Butler, toured with the Welsh team to Argentina in 1968; Eric Watts won a youth cap but turned to rugby league before the union game saw the best of him; Denis Thomas, my first partner in the Llanelli team, is there in the faded photographs somewhere, as is the MCC fast bowler Jeff

Jones, not forgetting former world snooker champion Terry Griffiths!

A magnificent assembly of talent. Indeed few teams – apart from Bridgend, as J.P.R. consistently reminds me – could muster a strong enough challenge to topple us from our all-conquering throne. The battles against Bridgend seemed to last for an eternity. Somehow schoolboy rugby, especially when there are only a cluster of onlookers to witness the great deeds, brings out the worst in the partisan father, teacher and coach. Illtyd Williams, a much respected figure in Mid Glamorgan rugby circles and coach to Bridgend during one of the five matches I played against them, once displayed the intense emotion that often inspired parents to wave umbrellas and sticks angrily at referees, and he succeeded in getting the match abandoned. He had been quite vociferous from the touch-line and the referee had politely asked him to temper his encouragement with a little less oratory and a little more tolerance. Illtyd would have none of it and promptly told the referee where to hang his whistle. Of such sentiments diplomats are born, and the ref, who was by now a degree or two less tolerant himself, asked the tirading Illtyd to leave the field. There then followed a heated argument between the two as to whether the referee had a right at all to order any man, woman, child or dog from a public park. The matter could only be resolved by the most severe measure available to the referee, and he pointed both teams to the changing rooms.

J.P.R. at that time was a rather diminutive figure compared with the towering likes of me. But we were both picked to play for the Welsh under-fifteen schoolboy team against England at Twickenham. Twickenham? That vast arena, which I'd only seen on television and read about when the Welsh heroes of the fifties battled against the white-shirts of England? When the team was announced I bought three copies of the paper just to make sure that it wasn't a misprint, and though Brian Wall of the *South Wales Echo* in one of his articles had kindly said that 'BENNETT IS CERT FOR CAP', I still couldn't believe it. My mother spent days before the big trip worrying if I had enough clothes to take to London and my father kept talking about the winds of the big Twickenham stands that had destroyed so many full-backs.

We could have played the game in the changing rooms! I had never seen such huge quarters and the baths were as big as our front parlour. It was all a bit of a blur, though I have a faint recollection of going to see Charlie Drake performing the night before at a theatre and not being able to eat a thing from the time I left Llanelli until trotting out before the fifteen-thousand crowd on that magnificent turf. The various theories about the 'Twickenham swirl' were shelved after the first five minutes, mainly because the wind kept changing so much that I lost track of where to expect the next gust. We went on to beat the England boys by 11 points to 3 and the thrill of watching a drop goal of mine described by Peter West on 'Sportsnight' and getting a mention from the late Pat Marshall in the *Daily Express* as a promising 'Paul' Bennett topped the icing on a day never to be forgotten.

There were two other internationals to be played during that season and though hard-pressed in both the game, against Scotland at Galashiels and the return match with England at Rodney Parade, the Welsh schools team remained unbeaten. Conquering heroes we might have been, J.P.R., Allan Martin, Roger Lane, Wilson Lauder and the like, but we were reduced to mere mortal size by the committee at Rodney Parade who gave us a right ticking off for a mini drinking session during our visit to Scotland. I can't for the life of me remember whether I was guilty, and I can't imagine any self-respecting landlord serving a fresh-faced five-foot fourteen-year-old. However, the session did take place and we all made the honourable decision to plead collective guilt.

*

Though I had been overjoyed by the experience of playing for Wales, I still had a hankering for the round ball. During schooldays I had turned up for Llanelli Schoolboys on Saturday mornings and then for a local soccer team called the Rangers in the afternoon. After leaving school I must have played fairly well for the local Rangers because suddenly I became the focus of attention for several football league clubs. Cardiff City and Bristol Rovers were the first in the queue with written offers, but along came 'Jock' Gallacher, the father of Llanelli and Bradford Northern forward Stuart Gallacher and also my team-mate in the Felinfoel Youth rugby team. Stuart's father was a scout in the West Wales area for West Ham and he immediately offered me a month's trial with the Hammers. It would have been an opportunity that a thousand boys would have jumped at, but the thought of going to London away from Felinfoel horrified me, and after consultation with my father I turned the offer down. When Swansea Town, as they were known in those days, invited me to sign terms it seemed a more logical thing to do, but it didn't please Bob Bennett at all, simply because he preferred rugby, but more to the point – hated Swansea! However Trevor Morris the manager at the Vetch Field managed to persuade the family that my future was with Swansea.

I played for the Swansea Town Colts team three days after signing, against a highly successful Swansea Boys' Club side. It was one of those gruelling and hard-knocking cup ties and predictably I suffered a bang on the knee. The world of professional soccer seemed a lonely place as I limped home from Llanelli station, especially as I knew that all my friends were having a whale of a time in the Felinfoel rugby club house.

Indeed the choice between the two codes was made a few days later. I was due to leave for Swansea and the Vetch for another Colts game, but a knock on the door announced the arrival of the Felinfoel Youth boys, who had a cup game against nearby Pontyates. 'Come on, bugger the soccer, you're coming with us!' Though I had no choice in the matter I felt relieved and I knew then that my soccer-playing days were over. I'd felt during practices with Swansea boys that all my running and energy would never merit comparison with the ball skills shown by some of the young apprentices.

Nevertheless, to this day I have a strong interest and passion for soccer, and that hasn't pleased some of the Welsh rugby selectors. Watching rugby used to irritate me, though goodness knows I'll have to get used to it in the years to come, but whenever I've been injured or told to rest there is nothing I like more than slipping down to the Vetch Field and watching the Swans. I can watch the match as an objective spectator, something that is impossible for me to do if Llanelli are playing at Stradey. I remember one famous occasion when the selectors were about to pick a West Wales fifteen to play against the All Blacks and, though injured, I was in the running for a place. I don't think that the officials thought very highly of me when they discovered that instead of watching Llanelli playing Swansea, I'd gone twelve miles down the road to watch Swansea Town play a Fourth Division league match. It didn't go down well because the message came back!

The transition from schools to youth rugby wasn't particularly difficult. The village sported a youth fifteen and the success of Felinfoel Youth became headline news in the local papers for three seasons. I'd managed to sneak a game or two for the Youth before leaving school, but that practice was stopped when I turned up at Ammanford one afternoon only to be confronted by Danny Davies, a schools selector. 'What the hell are you doing here Bennett?' he bellowed. I was rather thankful to Mr Davies for the reprimand since the Ammanford boys, generally considered by us sophisticates from Felinfoel as a bit of a 'cowboy bunch', played like a collection of welterweights and our bus, making a hasty departure, was stoned by local supporters.

When you consider that the youth team of a small

village like Felinfoel could field three future senior Welsh Internationals, a handful of future Llanelli players and an assortment of schoolboy and youth caps, it doesn't seem surprising that we swept everything in front of us. Ironically Stuart Gallacher, Roy Mathias and Brian Butler were eventually to find their way into the professional code after playing for Llanelli. Stuart and Roy of course won their union caps for Wales and, as I've mentioned, Brian travelled to Argentina in 1968 with the Welsh team. My regular scrum-half in those early days was Clive Howells – indeed he partnered me for some seven years. He was a talented player and did as much as anyone to carry the Felinfoel banner. However, it was another Felinfoel product, Colin Davies, who was picked with me as a half-back partnership for the Welsh youth fifteen.

I can look back now with satisfaction at the scores Felinfoel Youth would rattle up against teams run by much larger celebrated clubs. Glamorgan Wanderers were dispensed with 50–0, Pembroke County 29–0, Carmarthen Quins 43–0, Swansea 33–3. I don't want to mislead anyone, we had our come-uppances as well, but generally the Felinfoel bunch were as good as any in the land and formed the nucleus of the Llanelli and District team, who in turn were just as dominant a force. Mind you, by that time we had Derek Quinnell to help us along a bit.

In my first season with the 'wage earners', I still had a lot to learn about the ways of the world. A poignant memory was my first drinking bout with the local rugby boys. We'd gone on an end-of-season tour to Nottingham and on the Sunday, as is the custom with so many teams, a 'communion' party was arranged. By the time two p.m. came round, the local afternoon closing time, the club steward came across to pull the blinds down.

I can remember feeling relieved, because I'd just about downed as much beer as any underage drinker could manage. The look of horror on the boys' faces, contemplating an early shutdown to the proceedings, was quickly erased as the steward turned round and said, 'That's all right boys, the blinds are only for the nosey outside. Carry on! We never close here.' They eventually found me a few hours afterwards tucked underneath some overcoats, happily dozing away. 'There you are Phil *bach*,' came the generous advice, 'you take it easy until you get a bit older.'

Being a bit on the diminutive side, or from the Iberian stock, as Carwyn James comically puts it, I've never been too interested in the physical aspect of the game. I've seen some cruel punishment dished out in my time, but one of the most amusing incidents was at St Helen's, Swansea, in a youth match against the old enemy – Swansea. Brian Butler, who was none too backward in looking after himself and in his younger days a bit of a wild one, was having a right old tussle with Alan Faull, a member of the famous Faull family of Swansea. A try was being scored at one end, but everybody's attention had been drawn to two figures chasing each other around the ground. The referee was totally nonplussed as he watched Brian chasing Faull all the way to the St Helen's scoreboard and kicking the poor old Swansea man's backside with contemptuous regularity. Eventually peace was restored, but Brian's reputation as a 'hard man' persisted and his uncanny talent for ending up where trouble brewed made him a prize acquisition for the League.

I recall another Butler incident. It was the second youth international of the season against the Midland Colts, and we'd heard that they had a giant of a man in the second row. Indeed when the Midlanders grouped together at the Beeston ground, the rumours were confirmed and into the changing rooms stepped a colossus. Nigel Horton was as big as he is now, and it always has been a pleasure to play *with* him rather than *against* him. However in this game it was quite evident that the Midland Colts were out to upset our rhythm. At the very first line-out Derek Quinnell sank to his knees, obviously

25

struck by an illegal blow. The second line-out call was for a short one, and Robert Feahy was the next victim. The forwards were incensed and quickly held a summit conference. The skipper was former London Welsh and Pontypridd forward Bill Davey and the only words that could be heard from the private meeting were Butler's instructions. 'Throw the ball to the back of the line-out and leave 'Orton to me.' Two minutes later Horton was staggering around the field obviously concussed, the victim of persons unknown, and took no real interest in the game after that. The match settled down after those incidents and we eventually beat them by 15 points to nil. My contribution to that game was two tries; one of the officials who'd missed the moment on his Kodak asked me to dive over the line after the game so that the moment could be immortalized on celluloid. No matter how pleased I'd been with my effort, all such thoughts were quickly brushed aside when I entered the Welsh changing room.

All heads were low, eyes staring at untied bootlaces with silence reigning. No one dared move a muscle because in the middle of the room was Ieuan Evans the Welsh coach, ready to give the boys one of the fiercest verbal lashings that I've ever heard.

'Sit down in the corner Bennett!' I didn't sit in the corner, I dived for it. Ieuan paced up and down between the dirty shirts and shorts and tore into all fifteen of us.

'I'm disgusted', he said. 'If I'd wanted to see a boxing match I could have stayed in the Amman Valley. I haven't come a hundred miles to see that sort of exhibition. I've no doubt that some of you are pretty proud of what happened out there. Well, you've made a big mistake, boys, you were a discredit to Wales, to your families and to yourselves. I'll have no more of it!'

We played three matches during that season. The first had been at Bridgend against the Welsh Secondary Schools, a team which included J.P.R. at full-back, Gareth Edwards at scrum-half and Allan Martin at lock. However, I nearly missed the game and very nearly cost Brian Butler and Eric Watts from the village their caps. Again we were to be on the receiving end of the tongue of Evans the coach.

I'd arranged for a friend of mine to call for me and take me down to Llanelli Town Hall on his Honda. He'd promised to pick me up at five o'clock so that I would have sufficient time to meet one of the local Youth selectors Bryn Richards who was going to drive myself, Brian and Eric to the Brewery Field. The clock sped on to twenty past five, and there was still no sign of my friend. I dashed up to his house and there he was fast asleep in an armchair. By the time he'd woken up, we realized it was far too late for us to make Mr Richards' car. I walked home slowly and, since I'd only been picked as a reserve, I rationalized the matter away as just one of those things.

As soon as I got home, the door flew open and a very irate Mr Richards told me to get my bags. Where had I been? What bloody Honda? ... He then told me that I was playing because the original choice Peter Rowe had withdrawn. Inside Mr Richards' car were Brian and Eric, and I'm sorry to this day that I nearly lost them their caps. The lashing I got from Ieuan Evans when we eventually arrived was more of a tirade than a telling-off.

We lost the game by 6 points to 3. J.J. Williams, then at outside-half, dropped two goals and I don't think (as I've repeatedly told him) that he could drop another two if he played until 1990!

Compared with the 'boxing match' against the Midlands the final international encounter against the French youth team was more of a war. I don't think that I've ever played in such a dirty match. From start to finish there were punches thrown and players kicked on the floor. Strangely enough it was the first match that my mother had seen me play in and, much to my father's embarrassment, she kept on shouting, 'Leave my Phil alone, don't you hurt him.' It was also the last game she saw, and clearly it wasn't the type of match that I could take my two boys to see. The French prop had to leave the field after only a few minutes. Brian Butler and Mel James (later of Swansea) were in the thick of matters, and then I became involved. I had just minored the ball when up popped the French scrum-half swinging his boot straight into my face. Pandemonium broke loose, it was quite chaotic. The Welsh scrum-half Brian Mills went after the culprit; Brian Butler took off and seemed to take on the French pack singlehanded and, with the crowd encouraging him and the others on, the match deteriorated into a Glasgow gang scuffle in the middle of Stradey park. I don't know what Ieuan Evans must have thought, but I'm sure he'd seen nothing like it in his life. I remember later in the game scoring a try, but being forced to side-step off my right foot because by this time my left eye had closed and vision to that side was non-existent. Two of the players ended up in hospital and the papers the next morning made sordid reading.

I remembered that swinging boot of the French number nine for some time and years later in a match against France at Parc des Princes I looked at the programme and there was the culprit once again – Richard Astre. At the after-match function I sought him out, and when he saw me from a distance I called over, 'Come here you little bugger.'

By the look on his face, his memory was as clear as mine.

3

Llanelli

I had spent the week nervously walking around the house, pestering my father for more details about the forthcoming trip. It was a vision come true, a promise of a visit to St Helen's, Swansea, to watch the Scarlets take on the old enemy – the Swansea 'jacks'. I'd listened often to old men talk of past battles, some that should have never have been lost, nearly all of them 'morally' won. My father was no exception to that brigade of Llanelli supporters who only on the rare occasion would be-grudgingly acknowledge the presence of any other team on the field.

I had visited Stradey Park several times, either in the company of father and Uncle Thomas John or sometimes as a 'private' in the 'over the fence bandellero army' of nine-year-old nonpaying Scarlet devotees. But a trip to Swansea? . . . I was changed, washed and ready before eight a.m.

The platform at Llanelli General was a sea of red caps, scarves, mufflers and cloth caps. It was a massive pilgrimage which had left villages and homes deserted of menfolk. St Helen's, I thought, could never accommodate this moving mass of miners, steelworkers, teachers, ministers and boys. They were all good-humoured; the bantering, the jokes, the bets, everything adding to the excitement of the afternoon.

It was a Derby spectacular, hard, rough and uncom-promising. Skirmishes on the field started fights on the terraces; the shouting and the noise was incredible and

I kept tight hold of my father's jacket.

Swansea were leading by 5 points to 3 in the second half, with precious few minutes to go before the end. Suddenly Carwyn James at the outside-half made a half-break and passed to his centre Denis Evans. Evans gave the ball to Goff Howells and by that time there was sufficient room for Goff to round his man in the corner and race for a try underneath the posts. The conversion was as good as there. St Helens went mad! Hats, programmes, bags and newspapers were flung into the air. Some five thousand Llanelli supporters had witnessed one of those Scarlet miracles.

The journey home went all too quickly. Smiling faces everywhere, and each one of my father's friends trying to outdo the other in recalling every move of the afternoon's battle. I knew at that time that if ever I had the chance, I would become a Llanelli player. There could be no other club. There were other battles to be savoured at Stradey.

I can easily recall the visits by Cardiff. Here was a club that oozed with tradition. They were in Welsh eyes the 'establishment' of the eastern area. Cliff Morgan and Rex Willis were the half-backs and I could hardly take my eyes of Cliff Morgan. It wasn't fashionable to like Cardiff, a feeling, I suspect, born of envy and jealousy. It was always said at Stradey that to play for Cardiff was three steps nearer to a Welsh cap. To watch them play in those days was nearly as good as having the Welsh fifteen on your doorstep, and there may have been little more than parochial malice in the Stradey sentiments. Funnily enough, a little of that feeling about the 'Blue and Blacks' still persists. I don't know why, maybe it's as a result of knowing that Llanelli for years didn't match the charismatic quality of the Blue and Blacks. In the decade that I've been associated with Llanelli, the club has improved its image a hundredfold.

The transition from youth to senior rugby started in my last season with Felinfoel Youth. Llanelli found themselves short of their normal complement of players because of a Welsh trial and asked me along for a game.

30

When the invitation was extended they conveniently forgot to mention that the opponents were Swansea of all people. My debut was quite inconspicuous and the only thing that I can recall of that game is that the Swansea fifteen were reduced to thirteen men by the final whistle, and the absent two were hardly the victims of nagging hamstrings.

Aberavon then came along and blooded me into their club. I think I completed about six end-of-season games for them before returning to Felinfoel. Happy as I was with Aberavon, somehow it didn't seem right travelling through Llanelli to get to another club, and by the beginning of the next season, though I had reservations, I opted for Llanelli.

No matter how much my idolatory of the club had been influenced by the magic of Carwyn at outside-half or the impeccable play of Terry Davies at full-back, the lightning pace of Ray Williams on the wing, and the mud and often blood-splattering heroics of R. H. Williams and Howard Ash, I wasn't absolutely convinced that they were the right club for me. The heart certainly ruled that I should travel no more than the odd mile or so down the road for my senior rugby. Nevertheless, Llanelli had become a very average club and, when they asked me, after my brief flirtation with Aberavon was over, to go with them to Italy on a close-season tour, I turned the offer down.

There were rumours that all was not well in the Scarlet camp. Teams that were selected bore no resemblance to the fifteens that took to the field. If a chosen player didn't turn up, a telephone call to any one of a dozen smaller clubs, Tumble, Llanelli Wanderers, New Dock Stars, Felinfoel, would make certain that the requisite number of players would be fielded. This hardly generated confidence in the ranks; I'd also heard tales of how Llanelli would travel to play London matches with only about eight of the players on the bus knowing each other. Pride, confidence and enthusiasm were qualities that the players of Stradey in those days rarely possessed. There were times when the Wasps, the UAU and teams that should have been sent east with their tails hanging actually gave the Scarlets a run for their money and on the odd afternoon took the Sospan scalp. But during the summer a number of changes took place on the administrative committees of Llanelli and I sometimes wonder, had not these taken place, whether Llanelli would have become the magnetic force that they were in the late sixties and early seventies.

Peter Rees, who had won two caps for Wales in 1947, was elected chairman. His first move was to ask Tom Hudson, a physical education lecturer at Bath University, to get the Llanelli players fit. Tom was one of those fanatics who adamantly refused to believe that people played rugby to get fit; the reverse was the Hudson theory. He set about designing a course that the modern-day SAS would have found much to their liking. It was what he loosely called a hardening-up process; some of us tended to disagree, and would have been quite ready to commit Mr Hudson to an institution there and then.

A five-mile run was followed by the most remarkable exercise that I've ever witnessed. We were confronted by twenty trees, all of which – according to Tom Hudson – desperately needed tackling. Trees? Some of us exchanged glances of disbelief. Was this bloke for real? I mean, you could permanently damage yourself. A kick up the backside dismissed all thoughts we might have had of a walk-out protest, and soon a string of Llanelli players was to be seen diving into wooden stumps. Keith Hughes, the Llanelli and London Welsh centre, took one look at this unbelievable sight, then took another look and declared that if any Stradey supporter had witnessed the same scene we would all have been branded a bunch of nutters. In fact as the bodies writhed on the ground floored by the wooden opposition there were two old men on the sidelines, watching all this. They didn't say much, just looked at each other, shook their heads, continued with their stroll, wondering what time our keeper would return to lock us all up again.

Tom Hudson, despite all the lunatic antics, achieved his goal and that was to get us fit. The other influential factor was the election, as captain, of Norman Gale, a man of few words, but those few carefully chosen for effect. Norman was a leader who at once instigated a rule that all players had to be ready to play in the changing room forty-five minutes before kick-off.

Against this background of welcome upheaval I threw my lot in with Llanelli, and have never regretted the move since.

Llanelli have the only bilingual club scoreboard in the country and the decision to have Cardiff translated into Caerdydd and Swansea to Abertawe symbolizes the 'Welshness' of the club. The tea ladies, the committee men, Bert Peel the physiotherapist, the car-park attendants and a vast section of the supporters are Welsh-speaking. If anything, the amount of Welsh spoken at Stradey is not a divisive factor, as it is in other parts of Wales, but in fact the complete opposite.

Most of the players have been brought up in the surrounding villages of Tumble, Pontyberem, Llangennech and Kidwelly, though regrettably the source of this Cymric well seems to be drying out. The Welshness appealed to me enormously, especially when one played inside the likes of John 'Bach' Thomas and Gwyn Ashby, two delightful characters who would always find something other than rugby to talk about when on the field. John, the coffin-maker from the Amman Valley, would always have a quip at the ready. He would watch rather than support his fellow comic Gwyn Ashby in the centre. Gwyn would make a run, get tackled in the process of wondering where John was and then, cantering back to position, would inevitably hear John accuse him of being *mas o bwff* (out of breath). Gwyn, still bemoaning the lack of support, would reply, 'So would you be if you were working night shifts like me!'

If these two johnny-boys had played alongside Ray

Gravell it would have been marvellous theatre, but I doubt if any of the coaches or captains would have appreciated it. Ray is of the same mould. An odd verse or two of a Welsh lullaby would reach me in the middle of a game against Swansea, and then 'Mynyddygarreg' would walk back from a tackle which had all of us wincing – *'Weles ti hwnna Phil Bach? Fe fites i e!'* ('Did you see that Phil boy, I ate him!')

Indeed I can't think of any centre that has enjoyed playing against Ray. In the changing room he can destroy a captain's pre-match speech with a quip against one of his fellow players. He has exasperated coaches to tears of frustration, running hand in hand with his fellow centre Roy Bergiers after being told to stick close together in the middle, but he is as essential to the morale of the Llanelli fifteen as the coach, captain and committee combined. It was a tragedy that we didn't have him on the New Zealand tour of 1977. Rugby needs its Ray Gravells. He could reduce the Llanelli changing room or the Welsh room under the north stand to tears. Always late, barging through the door, throwing his kitbag onto the bench and with a huge *'Shw Mae'* to everyone, he'd quickly give a recital of the latest release by Dafydd Iwan, a Welsh-language pop singer cum campaigner. During the latter years I suspect that Dafydd Iwan has been short of new recording material, judging by the monotony of Ray's impromptu concerts. When bedrooms were allocated on club tours, the first priority would be to get a room as far away as possible from Ray's cassette player, and on one occasion I remember finding Duncan Darch, who was then a new recruit to the Llanelli second-row ranks, sleeping on a hotel balcony in the early hours of the morning.

'It's that bloody Dafydd Iwan maniac in there, I can't take any more,' mourned the six feet four Darch!

Only one thing could upset Ray before a game. If he wasn't allowed to be the second out of the changing room, it would annoy him for the rest of the afternoon. He must have had some grand ideas of vice-captaincy embedded in that Welsh grey matter, but many a time when I've been confronted by a huge breakaway back-row forward, I've been happy to hear the shout from my left, '*Gad y diawl i fi!*' ('Leave the devil to me!') That kind of brotherly support is always welcome.

I've yet to meet such a worrier. Before each game he will seek assurance that his opposite number is of no consequence whatsoever. Nobody is spared the Gravell opinion poll, and he will roam around a dressing room constantly chattering about the psychological damage he's about to cause the opposite centres.

Of course, in the Welsh changing room there were those who were well used to the Gravell need for assurance. There is one classic tale to tell. Gareth knew how to get the better of Ray and before going out to meet the French he nearly had Ray foaming at the mouth. '*Grav, ti mynd i ladd nhw heddi*' ('You're going to kill them today Grav'). '*Bwr yr un cynta mewn i'r enclosure*' ('The first one, hit him into the enclosure'). '*Bydd y bois ma rhy soft i ti achan*' ('This lot are too soft for you'). And so the psychological oration went on until Gareth had Ray just about ready to commit hara-kiri on the field. Each Edwards phrase had been devoured as gospel and the nervous excitement of Ray could hardly be contained.

As luck or misfortune would have it, the very next Saturday Llanelli were playing Cardiff at the Arms Park, and Ray and Gareth were on opposite sides. Gareth, cunning as ever, immediately seized the psychological upper hand. As he bent down to put the very first ball into the scrum he signalled over to Ray waiting in the centre and insinuated that Ray was suffering from an excessive beer gut. The next scrum he shouted over 'Hey Grav, *ti'n dew bachan*' ('Grav, you're too fat'). This continual abuse had two effects on Grav. First he was perplexed. After all, this was the man who had inspired him to great deeds the previous Saturday, and here he was now calling him a fat slob. The second reaction was one of anger, and it was as much as any of us could do to stop Grav from running over and punching Edwards.

35

Gerald, who had been in that same Welsh dressing room but who was now opposite Grav in a Cardiff jersey, appealed to Gareth to stop the teasing tirade. He knew only too well that Grav, transformed into a raging bull by all this perplexing abuse, would be too much to handle if he ever did get the ball. I can still hear Gerald's appeal for sanity! As ever, Edwards had that grinning smile on his face at the end of the game, and Grav sought our assurance as to whether Edwards was really all right.

One of the other 'Welsh' characters was Roy 'Shanto' Thomas, possibly the unluckiest hooker in Welsh rugby. He had a permanent seat on the replacement bench in the Arms Park. I don't know how many times he sat there – I remember someone saying that it was over thirty – but with Jeff Young and then Bobby Windsor reigning supreme Shanto had to settle for the number two role. His tales of his native Penclawdd were as wide as his toothless grin. Whatever anyone else could claim for his home village, Penclawdd would better the claim by five times as much. The salmon, the coal, cockles and chips were bigger and better than anywhere else in Wales.

His challenges and boasts did get him into trouble at times. He once, for a bet, claimed that he could down a bottle of whisky at a short ten-minute sitting. No one was particularly interested, but somehow we managed to scrounge a purse of six pounds to see if he could complete the feat. A half-bottle gone, he had turned a pale colour; with only a few gulps left, his eyes were full of tears, his face an evergreen texture ... and defeat was nigh. He looked at the remaining challenge and pleaded with us that he was worthy of the prize, but before we could disagree with 'Penclawdd', the exit door had become a far more attractive proposition than the whisky bottle. Challenges from the toothless front row man were few after that episode.

No one could ever accuse Shanto of biting in the mauls or scrums. He'd emerge from the ground-floor battles, gasping for air without a tooth in sight. The only time I ever remember him with a full set was at the beginning of a tour to Japan with the Welsh team. I did one of those theatrical double-takes when I saw Roy step on the bus with a set of teeth that looked as if they'd been borrowed for the duration of the tour. They were clearly uncomfortably and his first attempt at speech brought the house down. The set were removed and placed in the kitbag, and they never did make an appearance after that.

There have been other men and players that have passed through Stradey to whom rugby is a vehicle for humour and athletic expression rather than a reason for living. Recently I have felt that the increasing seriousness of it all has passed an unwanted burden onto our younger players. Perhaps it's a sign of melancholy, but on training nights at Stradey I've watched a number of hopefuls turn up at the ground and, capable players though they may be, there is little of the humour about them that was once an indispensable quality. Perhaps it's the over emphasis on coaching, the drive for success and the fear of failure. The supporters, the committee, the media all want success, and the prospect of a third-degree cross-examination on a Monday morning by workmates allows little levity to enter the game. Regrettably ... the game in order to survive has to have its characters.

Norman Gale, the Welsh and Llanelli captain and hooker, always used to hate playing against Clive Rowlands, his contemporary in the Welsh team. As soon as Rowlands spotted Gale, the chatter would start and Clive, who is never short of a word or two, would infuriate Norman so much that this would inevitably result in a succession of penalties being awarded against Llanelli. Gareth Edwards was another who enjoyed the lighter side of the game. He noticed during one match between Llanelli and his club Cardiff, that I'd broken my nose, before every scrum he threateningly pointed to his nose, indicating that if he ever got hold of me further surgery on the old hooter would be needed. He'd then rush up to tackle me, but always stopped his hands a few inches from the face; then chuckling back to his position he would mutter, 'Lucky that time Phil, *bach*.'

John 'Bach', Ray Gravell, Clive Rowlands, Chico Hopkins, Gareth Edwards and Roy Shanto Thomas were all characters, and though every single one of them was a great competitor, they also possessed a sense of humour – an asset sadly lacking in today's rugby men.

If Peter Rees and Tom Hudson transformed Llanelli RFC into a better-organized unit, the trinity became complete with Carwyn James. Here was a man who had graced the field of Stradey when I was a boy. The supporters of Llanelli always argue that he would have won scores of caps if the Welsh selectors hadn't been so Cardiff-biased and chosen Cliff Morgan so much. Though I had watched him many a time brilliantly balancing through defences, and marvelled at the towering drop-goals sailing from his boot towards Burry Port, my first meeting with him was as a fifteen-year-old. After playing in the Llanelli schools invitational sevens tournament, Carwyn approached my headmaster and then my parents and asked them whether they would like me to go to Llandovery College for the rest of my education. It was a marvellous opportunity. Llandovery's reputation as a rugby-playing school was well known throughout Wales. At the time it didn't appeal to me, though I knew that my parents would have done everything to make my stay there an enjoyable one. Llandovery was not for me, however, and I must admit that I have regetted that decision ever since.

The college had obviously given Carwyn, who was the rugby coach there, sufficient opportunity to put his ideas into practice, and as soon as his influence began to be felt in Llanelli, which didn't take very long, the scene was set more for revolution than a transformation. As well as the tactics and the philosophy that he employed, other innovations he introduced were equally important. His attention to the well-being of his players was as telling as his analytical appreciation. The squad system became common practice, the training sessions were always varied, but for once the player was treated with respect. No longer were we required to face Saturday morning trips to Old Deer Park. It now became an overnight stay at a London suburb hotel. There was no economy on the meals given to the players ... sausages and peas were replaced by steaks, and the committee responded to his demands. A philosopher and personnel officer rolled into one, and an inspiring one at that. The players took to the new leader. Carwyn had an uncanny way of knowing each individual's moods, he always had time to listen and his knack for the humorous anecdote when everything else around was deadly serious, was a marvellous armament.

On one Saturday morning Llanelli were heading for Pontypool for a Welsh Rugby Union Cup match. Apprehensively we approached the Gwent valleys and came across our lunchtime hotel. The team pep-talk would be here. After making sure that each individual knew what was required of him, Carwyn emphasized the need for a running game against Pontypool, a team not known for their speed of action or thought behind the scrum, but a team which under the guidance of their coach Ray Prosser had one of the most formidable packs in the country. We didn't need reminding on that morning that fixtures between the two clubs had been broken off for some time for 'diplomatic reasons'. The press had been building up the cup-tie as the 'aggro' battle of the season, and quite a few of us were reticent about the physical tussle waiting at Pontypool Park. James explained the As and Bs of the situation and then looked out of the hotel window onto a sunlit lawn. 'I prayed to God that it would be a glorious day for running rugby, and look at it, and there's nothing that even Prosser can do with a hundred hosepipes to change matters!' The talent of the man with his non-conformist style of preaching the serious matter would reduce us all to sombre front-pew deacons, and then, with the acceleration of wit and timing, a small joke would ease the burden and tension and we would suddenly become fifteen players who were capable of enjoying our rugby once again. That particular match against Pontypool in the cup was as hard as any, but Llanelli played well and won.

It is in the aftermath of the battle that the player sometimes feels lonely. The supporters are well satisfied with the conquering spoils, the committee retires to gin and tonic discussions about the fat attendance bonuses of winning cup rugby, but the player with adrenalin spent is alone to make peace with his world. A word of well-meaning gratitude from authority is always welcome. Here again James was a master of diplomacy, and so too Syd Millar, the coach of the 1974 Lions.

After the cup game with Pontypool, the team had been joined by their wives at the very same hotel where we'd had lunch. The relief of winning was evident and the pints were going down a merry pace. In walked the coach, and the mere suggestion from one of the party that a meal would not go amiss brought forth the hotel manager with twenty steak and chips for the players ... and eighteen chicken and chips for the wives. You could almost hear the committee men at the bar gulp with astonishment. But the small decisions that James made with one wave of the hand won him the devotion of all those who played under his leadership at Stradey.

I have no intention of tabulating the successes of Llanelli RFC during the James reign. In fact much of the credit should go to Ieuan Evans his predecessor at Stradey, a man of strong Welsh socialist principles, a fiery tongue, but a warm and affectionate man. He was a strong disciplinarian, and left Stradey for St Helens. But for that, Carwyn might never have become the Lions coach. It was during the transition period from the Evans to the James reign that the Llanelli team of the seventies began to take form. It is sufficient to say that during that time the cup was won in four consecutive years, the championship won twice and during the past decade thirteen players have represented Wales.

LLANELLI

We had led the *Western Mail* championship for most of
my first season, with what was on paper an amalgama-
tion of a few old heads and some very inexperienced
players. However, motivated by Ieuan Evans, we needed
a win against Neath in the final match of the season to
make sure of the title.

The Gnoll and the reputation of the Welsh 'All Blacks'
is a terrifying prospect at the best of times, but with the
added incentive of the championship title as well, the
match had intriguing dimensions. It was, to put it
bluntly, a rugged affair – Alan John one of our flankers
had to leave the field with a broken collar bone, Marlston
Morgan the other flanker broke his nose, but played on –
as did Stuart Gallacher, who later discovered he'd
broken his foot.

Whatever mathematical combination one uses, we
only had twelve fit men on the field of play but somehow
we scraped home by 9 points to nil and the title was
ours. The foundation had been laid and the successes, as
is so often the case, led to further success. The enjoyment
of the cup runs was further enhanced by the type of
rugby that we played. The stopwatch methods introduced by Carwyn were always evident as the ball was
sped from the base of the scrum to the wings; the option
of the crash ball was an effective decoy, and the forwards
soon got the message that transferring the ball from the
maul to the wings at a brisk pace would always create
opportunities.

However enjoyable the days of triumph were at Stradey,
they also brought their problems. I don't think that the
set-up at Llanelli was ready for the spotlight that was
inevitably focused on the club. There were committee
men there who became far too arrogant and cocky for the
club's good. People began to resent Llanelli RFC. I
suppose that in some ways, it was to be expected, but it
was hurtful to the players concerned to hear 'rumours'
about Llanelli that were completely false.

We were accused of 'poaching players', but I cannot

41

think of a single player who joined Llanelli who was unfairly persuaded to join. There were references to 'boot money' that allegedly placed some of the better players in the super-tax bracket! If that was the case, then somewhere along the line my income was being docked by persons unknown. What *is* true is that players did receive expenses for travelling to and from matches and training sessions. There is nothing under the counter about this practice, and how on earth the 'purists' in their ivory towers expected people like Peter Morgon *or* Paul Ringer to subsidize their own travel from Haverfordwest and Cardigan three times a week I'll never know. I know for a fact that the three weekly journeys from Llandysul to Llanelli, a distance of some forty miles, did place a strain on Clive Griffiths, and I personally think that it had a lot to do with his going north after his fleeting appearance in the Welsh jersey.

The committee during that golden span of years didn't really help matters. Some of them suggested strengthening the fixture list and dropping the less fashionable clubs; because of this selfish attitude I remember reminding some of them that the big clubs had to show humility during the successful years because no one knew what the future held and overnight changes of policy could often have far-reaching consequences. One particular incident when J.J.'s teeth were re-arranged during a match between Llanelli and Newbridge led to the cancellation of matches between the two clubs. Newbridge at the time had suffered a major gas explosion in their clubhouse and they faced the prospect of having to rebuild not only the structural walls that had been damaged, but also their image. I can remember some of the Newbridge players telling me that if clubs such as Llanelli started dropping fixtures with them then they would perhaps never be able to rebuild a good reputation in Welsh rugby. Success came to Llanelli at a fast and furious pace and, ironically, the damage it caused may have been more considerable than some people imagine.

There was certainly a great deal of resentment. In

some cases it was blatant hatred. The action of a well-dressed man sitting in the Abertillery stand will illustrate the point. We'd been drawn against Abertillery in the cup and, though the players and committee of the Gwent Club had made us feel very welcome, sections of the crowd were hostile. I had to run back and cover one kick; since there was little time to pick up the ball, I fly-kicked the ball into touch. The pinstripe-suited and sheepskin-coated Abertillery supporter stood up in his seat and shouted 'You f— cripple, I hope you break your back.' I can never understand such supporters, and however hard I try to rationalize them as the penalty to pay for our success, rugby could do without such malicious bigotry.

There is always the compensating factor though, and I'll never forget a conversation that I had with Gerald Davies after Cardiff had beaten us at the Arms Park in the cup. It was the first cup tie that we'd lost and I suppose that I was a bit down in the mouth. But the Cardiff club had asked me to go over to their clubhouse for a presentation. It was a marvellous gesture but Gerald, sensing that I wasn't feeling in a celebratory mood, asked me what was wrong. I explained to him that defeat after such a long run was a bit difficult to comprehend. 'You know.' said the Cardiff captain, 'I was watching the television the other night and Arthur Ashe was being interviewed after losing in the finals of a big championship match and do you know what he said when he was asked how he felt?'

'No,' said I, wondering what on earth was coming.

'Well,' said Gerald, 'Ashe looked at the interviewer and told him that the sun would rise in the morning, his kids would be all right, his wife would be there and another day would begin.'

He was right, I thought to myself. Pat and the kids will be all right tomorrow. It made sense. After all, it had only been a game of rugby – a sport that I played to enjoy. Looked at from Arthur Ashe's point of view, this triviality of a defeat meant very little at all.

Even in 1981, I had mixed emotions when we lost once again to Bridgend in the WRU Cup semi-final.... I had hoped to round off my career with a final appearance at the Arms Park in the Cup Final. Of course there was disappointment, that was only natural, but yet I could rationalize that it had merely been a game. It was really only something that you did because you enjoyed doing it. But then it's taken me a long time to get such matters into perspective. Gerald with his Arthur Ashe quip has helped me to do that.

4

Wales – 'Follow me quietly'

'Follow me quietly,' three words that instilled some badly needed confidence in me as I joined the Welsh squad for the very first time. The advice, readily given, came from Delme Thomas, who achieved more by deed on the rugby field than many would credit. How else does a man earn the respect of the McBrides and the Meads of the rugby world. He took it upon himself to make my entry into the higher atmosphere of Welsh rugby as painless as possible. Follow him I certainly would. Quietly? I was as dumb as a groom on his wedding morning!

I suppose I did feel all the traumas of a school beginner on that first occasion. The novel enjoyment intermingled with apprehension, the nagging worry of failing to do what was required – it was a day of high-pitched excitement. There were the 'sixth formers' of the new school, Brian Thomas of Neath, Denzil Williams of Ebbw Vale and Brian Price of Newport, names and faces that had adorned scrapbooks of mine. John Dawes was the captain and, under the watchful eye of David Nash the coach, I simply did what I was told and tried not to make myself conspicuous.

The outside-half position was occupied by Barry John, who was at that time beginning to mould his successful partnership with Gareth. They'd already been together for half a dozen games and that 'you throw it and I'll catch it' combination had an impregnable aura about it. I was simply content to occupy the sidelines – and

45

what better apprenticeship could there have been.

Ten years later I was to see some of those faces in the Welsh changing room at Dublin, completely drained of emotion and energy after one of the dirtiest international matches that I've ever seen or played in. The decade had taken its toll, success and continued success had made urgent demands on the chosen few and the enthusiasm was on the wane. Gerald's career on the wing had spanned a dozen years, Gareth had enough Welsh jerseys to clothe three fifteens, and Dr J.P.R. could recall more sporting injuries than any medical dictionary published.

Great players as they were, there were others who in those ten years had given their all to the Welsh cause. The successful seventies brought a strong bond into the Welsh changing room and the fact that the team was little changed during those years bears witness to the fact that here indeed was an amazing fraternity of talented sportsmen. Bobby 'Duke' Windsor had introduced badly needed scrummaging technique into the squad and with it his two illustrious colleagues from 'Pooter'; Allan Martin towered in the Welsh line-out, and then there was a host of talented backrow players: Dai 'Shadow' Morris, John 'Basil Brush' Taylor, the unique 'Merv the Swerv' and the inspirational Terry Cobner. The list is impressive, and if others behind the scrum tended to dominate the headlines on a Monday morning, they would be the first to acknowledge the unflagging efforts of a magnificent and durable set of forwards who saw Wales through the seventies.

I'm only glad to have been part of it.

Those early encounters with international rugby are shrouded in a haze of bewilderment. However, being 'carpeted' by Bill Clement, the Welsh Rugby Union secretary is an experience that no one is likely to forget. Delme, Norman Gale and myself had decided to travel to Cardiff airport together before flying to Dublin for the Irish match. We were summoned before Mr Clement.

'How come I have three separate claims for expenses in front of me, from Llanelli to Cardiff, when I know that you came together in the same car?'

He's got eyes in the back of his head, has Mr Clement. I wouldn't have dared question the prosecution at that time, but Norman seized the opportunity to give one of the finest orations on behalf of the working class that I can ever remember.

'Are you questioning our integrity over a miserable pound or two?' And before Mr Clement could answer, Norman explained to him how many ' — days' work' he'd lost because of 'the — match', how much overtime had gone up 'the — spout', how his mates had to fill in for him while he was 'kicking a — rugby ball' around some 'Irish — rugby field'. Of course he had my wholehearted support since I was losing nearly forty pounds in wages myself that weekend. But generosity has never been the hallmark of the Welsh Rugby Union.

It was Norman's alertness that won me my first cap in 1969, against France. We had both been selected as substitutes for Wales, and as the game progressed we had resigned ourselves to a quick shower, when suddenly Gerald in the dying minutes of the game was injured and it didn't look as if he could carry on. The call to action came so unexpectedly that in my fidgeting excitement the zip on my tracksuit trouser became stuck. There was little I could do about it, but pull at the damn thing and listen to Norman shout at me 'Get on quick, there are only a few seconds to go.' Suddenly he lunged at my tracksuit bottom, tore it to bits and there I was trotting out on the Stade Colombes pitch for my very first cap and into the history books as Wales' first-ever substitute. I think during those dying minutes Barry had the ball once and he hoofed it, without ceremony, down the field. I hadn't touched the ball in my first international; it had all passed in a flash, and I was still panting after the frustration of battling against my tracksuit zip.

The after-match celebration was made that much more enjoyable because of that brief appearance. The dinner was honoured by the presence of President Pompidou, but the likes of Denzil Williams and Brian Thomas were on hand, and to them protocol and decorum sounded something akin to an anti-flu bug. Each Welsh player was asked to do a turn or issue a demand of his fellow players. Maurice Richards, one of the most talented wings ever to grace a Welsh jersey, was a devout Christian, and the nearest I'd ever come to a teetotaller since leaving Adulum Chapel. However the French vineyards had done the trick, and the burgundy had taken over. When his turn came, without hesitation, he asked everyone wearing false teeth to place them in a water jug that he was holding at the head of the table. It was amazing how many extractions took place that night, and suddenly the water jug was full of the produce of dental technicians from Blaenavon to Bynea. It was indeed an ugly sight, but the President, pointing to his head to suggest that we all needed head surgery, some-how managed to finish his port and took the spectacle in great humour.

I'm sure that Ian Fleming when he pictured his 'Bondian' character, Oddjob, had somebody like me in mind. A cap on the wing against South Africa, in the centre against Scotland and eventually, after the 'King' (Barry John) abdicated, in my natural position at outside-half. Thankful that I was to have been picked at all, I shall never understand why I was ordained on the flank. The apprehension was shared by the two Welsh locks against South Africa, Delme and Geoff Evans of London Welsh, and I was taken to a corner to work out some line-out tactics.

Again it was Delme who offered the advice. 'Now, as soon as you see me blink, throw the ball in low and hard.' I'd never thrown a ball into a line-out in my life, but the instructions seemed quite reasonable; however, Delme's facial contortions before every line-out always included about half a dozen winks, and the South Africans were as surprised as some of my Welsh colleagues to discover how unprofitable the Welsh tactics were that afternoon!

In that first season Wales suffered mixed fortunes. The ill-fated 1969 tour of New Zealand which is described elsewhere had seen off a number of the hardy old heads and there were selection problems behind the scrum. Gareth seemed ill at ease with the burden of captaincy, though he insists to this day that he was a better captain than many credited. His track record shows that he only lost four matches out of thirteen as skipper and there are few around with such tales to tell. But at the time he reminded me of Clive Rowlands, a rugby pentecostal, fired by the word and damning all those who didn't accept.

I still felt with some justification that I was very much a fringe character, a feeling that was enhanced when I was justifiably dropped after the Scotland game which Wales had won fairly comfortably by nine points. Wales then went to Ireland, and were sent back across the Irish channel with their heads bowed after a convincing defeat. But the Welsh were on the verge of greatness: several of the young 'striplings', Gareth and Barry, Gerald and John Bevan, Mervyn Davies and John Taylor, not forgetting J.P.R. at the back, were beginning to acquire that presence of mind that is nurtured by experience.

Bill McClaren during his match commentaries often refers to certain players having time to perform their functions on the field with ease. That is not so much a matter of skill, but confidence. An international game is no place to show signs of stress and panic, there has to be a calm inside that will dominate your own performance. There have been players who have come and gone who would always win Eisteddfodic competitions for passion and *hwyl*, but during the past decade Wales had been fortunate to possess characters who had the ability to retain all their faculties upstairs when the rub of the green has been against them. I can recall Barry John's run through the French defences at the Stade Colombes in 1971, J.P.R.'s drop-goal for the Lions in New Zealand in the same year, Gareth's defensive kick from his own

twenty-two metre line against England in the 1978
Twickenham mud, and Gerald's last-minute pass to
Terry Cobner against the Scots at the National Stadium.
Indeed, more recently, Gareth Davies's massive relieving
kick against the French in Cardiff in 1980. And who
could ever forget the irascible grins on the faces of the
Pontypool twins, Charlie Faulkner and Graham Price,
when they scored their tries for Wales against Ireland
and France ... only to be matched by the famous
toothless smile from 'Cobs' when he was, as ever, on
hand to tail the ball from Gerald for a try against the
Scots. These are the moments to savour.

In the final match of the 1970 season, John Dawes was
selected as the Welsh captain, a man whose reading and
perception of the game I had admired in Argentina in
1969. Against the French I was chosen at outside-half
and in no uncertain manner John gave me my instructions for the afternoon.

'Now then Phil, I don't want to see the ball all
afternoon, just put it down there on the French line, and
keep it there.' There were times that afternoon when a
run in the threes was on, but one look at John put all
such thoughts out of my head. His one concession came
in the second half, when he asked me to put the ball
behind the French backs. The tactic worked, because
we stifled the French and chalked up an 11 points to 6
win.

At the time I knew I had an outside chance of selection
for the 1971 Lions. Various signs and whispers had been
sent down the grapevine, and having Carwyn, the Lions
coach, at Llanelli kept me in the limelight. Whatever
chance I had, though, was swept aside by the touring
Fijians. Years later Carwyn admitted that I would have
toured New Zealand but 'Gosforth cost you the trip, Phil
bach.' Gareth, J.P.R. and myself had been selected to
play for the Barbarians against the Fijians. J.P.R. as
usual gave his usual titanic display but the rest of us
were a disgrace. We showed no commitment whatsoever
and the Fijians scored a notable victory. I had an

exceptionally poor game – if ever there was a match that I would love to forget that one would rank highly. It cost me the Lions trip and the number two place to Barry.

A year later at Stradey, it was some consolation for me to beat a number of the All Blacks that I would have met on the tour. I was to meet them again during their 1972 tour of the British Isles. In retrospect I think that the Llanelli defeat probably did more to sour the emotions between the All Blacks and the public than most factors. I know that matters were not well in the visitors' changing room at Stradey, and even during the first few weeks there were rumours of cliques in the touring side; there were indications that the 1972 New Zealand All Blacks were suffering from weak management.

In the match against Wales, they deserved to win, despite the fact that their *enfant terrible* Keith Murdoch grounded the ball before reaching the line. Why is it that matches between the Welsh and the All Blacks create such controversy? From the Deans try to the Haden 'fall-out' in 1978 the games are hardly ever remembered for their quality, but instead for questionable incidents. Wales have come off second best to the All Blacks on too many occasions for the supporter who has been fed on success in the 'European theatre', and for our divine sovereignty to be questioned so frequently has generated resentment. Through the good management of their 1978 touring party in Wales, a little 'sweet reasonableness' emerged, to the eternal credit of manager Russ Thomas and captain Graham Mourie.

Against Wales in 1972 it was a different matter entirely. That night Keith Murdoch is alleged to have been involved in a squabble with an Angel Hotel security guard, and was sent home. I am in no position to ponder on the merits of the case, but I know that there had been other regrettable incidents before the Angel bust-up. It must have been a difficult decision, a shattering experience for the touring party, and from that moment on they didn't want to know about Wales or the Welsh supporter.

Be that as it may, in their penultimate match of the 1972/73 tour, before their game with the Barbarians, they gave one of the most convincing displays of running rugby that I've ever seen. They swamped the combined Neath and Aberavon team by a merciless score of 43 points to 3. But my appreciation of the touring team's abilities was soured by the attitude of some Welsh supporters towards them. Young boys jeered them, older men cussed them, the language was foul, the hatred intense. The rugby men in black humiliated the home side, but the behaviour of the Welsh that day humiliated our good name in rugby. When will people realize that despite the intensity of the game, it is after all a game to be played by men who have wives, children, homes and overdrafts like everybody else.

That kind of behaviour was evident again in a few days' time. Sections of the crowd jeered Sid Going when he was forced to leave the field against the Barbarians. Whatever caused this bitter feeling against Ernie Todd's All Blacks had seeped through to the core. Mercifully 'that game' will be remembered for better things than the immature prejudices of a few.

Again my feeling of being on the perimeter of matters returned when the Barbarians assembled for their pre-match workout. Most of the triumphant 1971 Lions had been picked. John Dawes was the captain and, though the Barbarian committee disliked intense preparation, Carwyn James was there ready to be consulted if need be. I felt estranged since the match was obviously being billed as the 'Lions of '71' against the 'All Blacks of '72'.

I remember the training session quite well since I nearly didn't get there. 'Could you direct me to the Penarth rugby ground, please?' I swear that forty-nine of the fifty people that I asked didn't know that such a place existed.

From the moment the players took to the field at Penarth I knew that pride was at stake, but John Dawes convinced us that a win against the tourists would not be achieved at the expense of enjoyable rugby. Even

Carwyn, admitted by the back door, told us to 'take them on, but to enjoy ourselves'.

The events of that match have been well chronicled and kept on tape for posterity's sake. It has been claimed as the match of the century, and yet I don't think that the All Blacks have been credited for the contribution they so readily gave to that feast of open play. As for that first try? Typical of Edwards to be 'snip watching' as usual and taking a pass that was meant for John Bevan on the wing! I don't think that the try would ever have been started unless I'd heard Alistair Scown's threatening feet right upon me; my side-steps were really exercised in order to get me out of trouble. But when you see an English hooker calling for the ball and willing to run as well, these are moments which mustn't be forsaken for a safe kick to touch!

If that tour was marred by incident, the dinner after that game was a credit to the brotherhood of rugby. The Barbarians' president Brigadier Glyn Hughes tried valiantly to continue with his speech but was somewhat overshadowed by the presence of Willie John McBride on the table giving the whole audience his copyright version of 'Galway Bay'. Above all, there was the satisfaction that night that we had achieved something special. It had also, so I thought, established my right as a worthy heir to 'King' Barry John's throne.

I had mixed feeling when Barry retired. I knew that it would give me and others the opportunity of competing for the outside-half position, but on the other hand I was surprised that he had given up so early. His understanding with Gareth was uncanny, and his easy-go-lucky charm hid a great competitive spirit inside. The 'calling' to the financial and broadcasting world was irresistible and selfishly, I suppose, I was relieved.

That relief quickly disappeared during the 1973 season, since it was a bad one. Supporters and critics urged me to run as I had done in the Barbarians game. The papers were full of 'Bennett must run, Bennett needs confidence,' and I could sense the crowd's anticipation whenever I had to gather the ball in a defensive position. All of which eventually probably did present me with a confidence crisis.

What those people didn't realize was that I was a relative newcomer in the Welsh side. The same demands were made of Gareth Davies and Terry Holmes when they first appeared, but it takes time and patience to generate the type of confidence required, and nothing gives me greater pleasure than to watch the maturity of the Davies and Holmes partnership blossom. Injury robbed Terry in the 1981 season of the chance to mature his partnership with Gareth in the Welsh team, and I have every sympathy with those two fine half-backs Gary Pearce and Gerald Williams, who had to bridge the gap during such an indifferent season for Wales. The pressure on Gary and Gerald was enormous, yet people expected them to transform the national fifteen overnight. Patience is a rare virtue when it comes to assessing half-backs in the Principality! The same can be said of any position, and the Welsh supporter owes a great deal to the selectors, who have over the years allowed a number of players the time to establish their right in the national fifteen. There has basically been nothing wrong with English rugby over the years apart from impatient petulance in the selection system. I sometimes wonder if Barry, Gareth and myself would have received such latitude if we'd been born on the other side of Offa's Dyke.

Running courageously against opponents, wrong-footing the first vanguard of defence, looks attractive to the hipflask-carrying debenture-holder, but he'll be the first to call for blood if you suddenly slip in an exposed position and the opposing back-row are able to make capital of your misfortune. Modern rugby, especially since the change of laws relating to kicking outside the 'twenty-two', has placed greater emphasis on support play and the player needs to assess all the options before committing himself and others to a great deal of needless defensive work.

Tactically the 1973 season was a disaster. We tried to

run the ball against the Scots but were caught out by a typically dour but rugged Scots defence, the French outkicked us, the Irish ran us close, and the only team to feel the wrath of the Dragon's tongue was England. We were rather overcommitted to the crash ball and, though we possessed the flair, the moves had become stereotyped and far too easily interpreted by the opposition. After the disappointment of 1973 there was evidence of better times to come in 1974.

The papers were full of speculation as to who might travel to South Africa with the Lions team. I knew that I was in with a chance, providing that nothing went drastically wrong in the forthcoming season. I was beginning to settle down with Gareth, but yet again we failed to provide a convincing performance as a national fifteen. It was Scotland's turn to travel to Wales, and a debut try by Terry Cobner gave us a narrow win. Then we were more than fortunate to share the spoils in a 9 all draw against the dominant Irish pack in Dublin. Against the French I had something of a personal crisis before venturing on the field.

It was pouring on the Thursday afternoon as we collected together for a run-out at Sophia Gardens in Cardiff. The conditions were dreadful and several questioned the wisdom of having any kind of practice at all. By the time we'd finished, several of us felt quite miserable and indeed as I drove home to Felinfoel that night, I could feel the shivers. The next morning, despite feeling groggy, which I dismissed as early-morning tiredness, I travelled to Cardiff.

As soon as I arrived at the Angel Hotel, I told the selectors that I wasn't feeling a hundred per cent, and I must have looked the part because after the early-evening meal I was ordered to bed with some aspirins dug out of somebody's handbag.

In the morning that drowsy feeling persisted, but I did feel slightly better. Dr Jack Mathews, however, would have none of it.

'If he plays this afternoon there is a good chance he'll

catch pneumonia. His temperature is high and not only is he not match fit, he should be ordered home at once.'

I phoned Pat, my wife, who was staying with J.J. Williams's wife at Maesteg, and told her that I was on my way home. During the time when I was picking up my kit I heard that Keith James of Pontypool had been called up as a replacement, which meant that John Bevan of Aberavon had probably been told that he was playing.

I was about to jump into the car outside the hotel when a voice asked. 'Where do you think you're going?' There were two selectors there, who obviously knew nothing of my 'pneumatic' attack. I told them the story quickly, and then the two pondered awhile and, almost together, asked, 'How do you feel now?'

At that particular moment I didn't feel at all bad, which was sufficient reason for them to give me a 'hold all operations' command until they conferred with the other three selectors. In ten minutes I was in front of the committee and I explained to them, as I had done to Jack Young and Rees Stephens, that I was feeling much better.

'Can you play?' they asked.

'Yes.'

'Do you want to play?'

'Yes.'

A frantic phone call was made to Maesteg to cancel the previous arrangements and I took the field against the French that afternoon. I felt genuinely sorry for John Bevan and Keith James, who must have thought that I was a real jerk. Ironically, I had one of my better games for Wales and we came away with a credible 16 points all draw against the French. But I was to pay the penalty for my Lazarus act, being forced to spend the next four days in bed.

I had my sights now on a Lions tour, but I still needed a reasonable game against England to secure a place for South Africa. We lost at Twickenham in a match that will be remembered for J.J.'s disallowed try. What irked my Llanelli colleague and friend was the consensus of opinion among the England players that it was a genuine try. It would have won us the match, and it would have kept J.J. quiet for the night! As it was we were both relieved to find that we were bound for South Africa that summer.

The return from the triumphant Lions tour was indeed memorable but the 1975 rugby season in Wales for me is best forgotten, for tragic personal reasons. We lost our first child, and all the victories and scores and good times seemed insignificant. I was neither mentally prepared nor physically attuned for the 'unofficial' test match against New Zealand, and my involvement during the 1975 home international season can only be described as passive. John Bevan of Aberavon played against England and France but was unfortunately injured during the match against Scotland. I came off the subs' bench and had what I can honestly admit was a stinker of a game. It was my worst performance for Wales, and if the selectors had cut short my international career forever that afternoon, I would have had no complaints. There must have been 15,000 Welsh fans at Murrayfield to witness that defeat by 12 points to 10 and I tried my best to avoid each one of them that night. The Irish came to Cardiff for the final encounter of the season and quite inexplicably everything went right: we won handsomely and I had a reasonable game. The silver lining had appeared at last, and the reward was a place in the Welsh touring party to go to Japan.

I have never been a chronicler of records, but immediately before our match against Ireland at Dublin in the following season, acres of press had been devoted to the possibility of my breaking the Welsh points record. The possibility hadn't escaped my notice, but once on the field I forgot all about it. As ever, anything but concentration on the game against the roving Irish would have had dire consequences. During the second half there was a high tackle on J.P.R. and we were awarded a penalty. The backs wanted to run the ball, since we felt that we had the measure of the Irish defence. Mervyn Davies the captain, probably wanting to punish the foul with a certain 3 points on the board, would have none of it and called me over to take the penalty. I must have kicked a hundred like it, and it wasn't from a particularly difficult angle. No, I mustn't make excuses – it was a sitting target. But Bennett had to miss it, and as I, head down, trotted back for the re-start I could hear Merv muttering something which sounded like 'What a bloody idiot.' Only after the game did I realize that I had just missed the points record. It was symptomatic of that season. Being called a bloody idiot by your captain is bad enough, but being dropped from the Welsh squad altogether is far more traumatic. That tale of high drama appears elsewhere.

The Welsh team were unstoppable in the next, 1976, season, scoring a total of a 102 points and allowing a meagre 37 to go against them. The Grand Slam was won for the first time in five years, but my one abiding memory of that all-conquering quartet of victories was the courage of Mervyn Davies in the game against France. The French had stepped on him, and 'Swerv' had broken a blood vessel. Despite his obvious handicap he played on, and I'm convinced, had he gone off the field, we would have had to settle for a Triple Crown. It was typical of the man, and no one felt as sorry as I did when that head injury in the semi-final against Pontypool curtailed his career as the Welsh captain and in all probability deprived him of the captaincy of the 1977 Lions.

One of the most difficult pre-match speeches that I had to undertake was before the cup final between Llanelli and Swansea. Mervyn was still at Heath Hospital in Cardiff recovering from surgery and I knew that the Swansea boys would dearly have loved to walk down the hospital corridor to present their skipper with the cup. The Llanelli boys were very conscious that most of the crowd at the Arms Park on that day were sympathetic to the Swansea cause, and I had a devil of a job convincing them that Mervyn would want no part of the trophy at St Helen's unless it had been fought for with the maximum of competitive spirit.

The sequence of events had turned a complete circle. I had temporarily been thrown out of the Welsh squad by the selectors and I'd fought my way back in and been a part of a Grand Slam winning side. It's a haphazard world and, though you may have a string of caps to your credit, the uncertainty on selection day is still there. It always came as a relief to hear my name read out or see it in a paper. Somehow, no matter whether you were feeling on top of the world, you needed that confirmation. By the time that the 1977 season came round, we knew that Merv would never play again, a tragic loss not only to the Welsh team but also for the Lions touring team that would be selected at the end of the championship. The Welsh selectors were looking for a skipper to replace Mervyn.

The phone rang and at first I thought that someone had the wrong number; then I recognized Gareth's voice.

'*Llongyfarchiadau*' ('Congratulations'), he chirped and I thought he was wishing me a happy new year in Welsh.

'Same to you, Gar.'

'You're captain.' It took some time for that to sink in.

'What about Cobs?' I asked, knowing that Terry Cobner had led Pontypool for seven years.

'He's ill,' replied Gareth.

'Good God.'

It took some time for this new challenge to sink in and my first thoughts were of appreciation for Gareth. I knew how much that telephone call had cost him; he would dearly have liked the captaincy again, and would probably have relished the responsibility which had been a burden to him at the beginning of his career. I walked around in a daze, captain of Wales! Me! I was working for Courage brewers at the time, and had to make a few calls on Gower. It's a large, expansive common, the Gower, and I pulled the car into a lay-by, and stared at the dashboard, not knowing what to think.

My first priority was not to get injured before the first encounter with Ireland at the national stadium. I succeeded in that task and started to worry about my pep talk. I wondered how the other boys would react. Clive had pulled at the heart-strings: mothers in the stand, uncles and cousins in the enclosure, all calculated to rouse the passion. Gareth had been something like that as well; Sid Dawes was a tactical man making sure that we all knew precisely what to do. Merv had led by example, and I knew I couldn't hope to compete with the lyricism of a Willie John McBride – 'We'll take no prisoners, there is no retreat' – where on earth he got such immortal phrases I'll never know.

I managed to string a few words together, but the time went ever so quickly and suddenly the heat of the Irish pack was upon us. They played well for the first half, but the game changed around after the sending-off of Geoff Wheel of Wales and Willie Duggan of Ireland. The referee Norman Sanson didn't hesitate and I suspect that a directive sent to all referees to stamp out dirty play gave him no alternative.

When I rushed over to plead with him, Willie was already on his way to the showers. Norman turned around and told me that he'd warned them before that incident. Geoff was nearly in tears....

'Please don't ... please!'

I felt so sorry for him because I knew that the disgrace of an international sending-off would affect him deeply. The actual incident had looked worse than it was – just a punch and a slap. It annoyed me because I could witness far worse misdemeanours every Saturday afternoon and they went unpunished. According to the letter of the law Norman was right, but I couldn't help thinking that this was the man who had spent several weeks with Geoff Wheel, enjoying his company during the Welsh tour of Japan. The Irish were beaten but we were by no means satisfied with our performance.

We were even less satisfied with the French game –

indeed we lost. I still feel a selection error probably cost us the game, because we were murdered up front. Bobby Windsor apologized to me afterwards for the way the pack had played. Glyn Shaw had been recalled to the front row and, despite his obvious talents as a mobility player, his scrummaging was exposed that afternoon. It was by no means Glyn's fault . . . we simply weren't clued up for the game at all. There were a number of missed chances which, had they been taken, could have won the game for us, but it would have been a grave injustice.

There is nothing you can say to a team that has been outplayed, and the selectors were quite charitable about the matter. As soon as we arrived back at our Paris hotel, a few of us ducked around a corner and managed to find an empty bar. A couple of fellas from Swansea paid for the drinks and, as we were about to reach that stage when a post-mortem seems inevitable, into the bar ran Clive Rowlands dressed in his 'penguins'.

'I thought I'd find you here. The dinner has started, you know, and the bloody top table is half empty, Come on!'

At the dinner I made my speech, saying, I hope, all the right things, to a room which looked strangely deserted since half the Welsh team had already left for a Parisian tour.

Not to be outdone, a few of the Welsh 'loyalists' were later taken on a trip by Jean-Pierre Rives, a French national hero. He treated us to a fantastic evening, an unforgettable experience, made especially noteworthy when J.J. had to cough up £26 for a bottle of champagne!

You may gather from that rather unkind quip that J.J. is a bit slow in coming forward with the coin of the realm. The truth of the matter is that he finds parting with any money far more painful that the worst of pulled hamstrings. Before he accuses me of great hypocrisy let me hastily add that I had my moment of embarrassment that night as well. The difference is that I have very little recollection of my misdemeanour whereas parting with five fivers must have sent old J.J. into a fit. Rumour has it, and I only accept it as a rumour, that I clambered on the stage where Sacha Distel was going through his cabaret act and insisted that I sang to him. Again it is rumoured by those who had polished off more than J.J.'s champagne that I mumbled through the first line of 'I'm going home to Swansea town'. I can't even remember the second or third line in the cold light of day, so how on earth could I have had the audacity to walk up to Mr 'Golden Voice' himself to sing with him on the stage. No, I could never have done such a thing, could I?

Somehow the Jean-Pierre Rives travelling circus managed to get back to the hotel at 8 a.m. for an 8.30 a.m. bus to the airport. The departure from Paris was a disaster. The eyes weren't even adjusting to daylight, let alone seeing the signs and signals to our awaiting aircraft on the tarmac. Nearly half the Welsh team were left at the airport, while the officials were safely tucked away in the tourist compartment seats and bound for Cardiff airport. We watched the plane take off, and spent the rest of the day competing with the Welsh supporters for seats and trying to phone our wives to explain that we'd been let down by the Welsh Rugby Union once again. Again at the airport the French hospitality was superb and there was a somewhat cynical look on Pat's face when I eventually made it back home at seven p.m. that evening. No, it wasn't cynicism – it was downright anger. I quickly turned my thoughts to meeting England at the Arms Park in a fortnight. That option seemed, at the time, far more attractive.

There is something about the English press that worries me. It is their ability to label an England team with only a victory or two to their bow as world-conquering heroes. Give England a win and the scribes present them as fifteen hearts of oak who will die for St George and Merrie Old England. Someone should slip them the word that such sentiments have a marvellous effect on the opposition. Such was the case in 1977. England were on course for the Triple Crown and we had played badly against Ireland and France; hence the revival of

62

English rugby was much heralded.

I read the papers, as I knew the other Welsh lads would do as well, and I set my mind on my next pre-match speech. I thought that the Terry O'Connors and the David Frosts and John Reasons of the Fleet Street world might do it for me. I couldn't think of anything to say but as I travelled up from Llanelli on the train to Cardiff on the Friday I looked out of the window and the muse 'hit' me.

The next morning the Welsh fifteen were treated to a rare old nationalistic speech. 'Look at what these — have done to Wales. They've taken our coal, our water, our steel, they buy our houses and they only live in them a fortnight every twelve months. What have they given us ... absolutely nothing. We've been exploited, raped, controlled and punished by the English, and that's who you are playing against this afternoon.'

'Come on Gar, look at what they're doing to your fishing, buying up the rights all over the place for fat directors with big wallets. Those are your rivers, Gareth, yours and mine, not theirs.'

Dear me it was quite some speech I can tell you. But later that night after the England boys had been sent back to the drawing board once again, I turned to Gareth and asked if he thought it was a bit of a daft oration.

'Yes,' he replied quietly and smiled. I suddenly thought then that I'd been the biggest mug in creation trying to stir up a man who had the experience of forty-eight caps.

We had turned the corner against England and we had matured as a team. Scotland represented the final hurdle – if we won, another Triple Crown would be ours. It was that maturity that led to the downfall of the Scots. Wales were a lot calmer than the fiery Scottish lads, and a piece of Gerald Davies and Steve Fenwick magic in defence eventually led to my scoring a try under the posts. I've often been asked what my feelings were lying underneath the Scottish posts with the ball propping up my chin.

There were absolutely no thoughts in my mind at all ...
it was a gesture of sheer exhaustion, after a 'rabbit run' of
some distance.

The selectors were to pick the Lions team for the 1977
tour of New Zealand that weekend and several of the
Welsh team had won their places on that tour with that
Scottish performance. Perhaps you'll forgive me if I
dwell on the merits of that selection and the events of
that tour in a later episode. The return of the 1977 Lions
was greeted by a wake of analytical post-mortems. It was
all quite extraordinary, and the scribes went to ground in
order to beat each other to the presses for 'the' authori-
tative account of our failure against the All Blacks.

It had a spill-over effect on the Welsh team, who had
contributed so many players to the tour. We could be
written off, said some; we were over the hill, said the
others. Some of us, it's true, may have been a bit old in
the tooth, but nothing can so stir a man to gird his loins
as to be called a veteran in the morning dailies. By the
time some of the New Zealand books had appeared in the
High Street shops and the reasons for our failure had
been psychoanalysed to the nth degree it was time to face
another domestic international season. For the opener,
Wales had to cross the border to face England and the
conditions were so reminiscent of New Zealand – they
were awful.

Cold driving rain and a field fit for a rice farmer.
Twickenham has never looked so miserable and England
were well equipped up front to compete in heavy going.
It wasn't a penalty kick or a try that beat them on that
day but one of those Edwards 'specials' – a low-
propelling diagonal tactical kick into the wind – and the
rain that drove the English pack back to their own
22-metre line. We were awarded a penalty shortly afterwards and I remember looking around for our two
recognised kickers, Steve Fenwick and Allan Martin;
strangely they both had their backs to me! It was a vital
kick and, fortunately for me it went over and we came
away from HQ with a 9 points to 6 win. It was a

satisfying victory mostly because several of the pundits had got it so very wrong.

The next hurdle saw the Scots come to Cardiff, and on paper a 22 points to 14 victory appears to be a comfortable afternoon's work. Far from it. The Welsh team had achieved something of a professional plateau to its game and anything short of that simply wasn't good enough. We played below par against the Scots, attempting the crash ball through the middle too often. There were also arguments on the field and Gareth tried to go on his own too often, for which he later apologized. Anybody entering the dressing room after the match would have been forgiven for thinking that we had lost by a colossal amount. Such was the frustration of knowing that we had failed to realize any of our potential.

To win the Triple Crown is an achievement that I don't think I will appreciate for years to come. I wonder what the children of Steven and James will say when they realize that their grandfather played in a team that gained such a distinction. However before the three crowns became a reality, Wales had to travel to Ireland and Landsdowne Road, a green quicksand for aspiring Welsh Triple Crowners. It was a dirty game, which I have no doubt accelerated my retirement decision.

As is the custom, the referee Monsieur Domercq went to knock on the Irish changing-room door to ask if their captain John Moloney was ready to toss a coin and choose ends. The door was slammed in his face and I thought, 'O God, there's something going on here!'

My worst fears were justified because the Irish on that day used a little more force than was necessary and left several of the Welsh team bewildered at such animosity from players who had been colleagues on Lions tours. It was quite frightening and, despite several appeals to the Irish to keep calm, the match degenerated into an unsightly affair between two teams that should have known better. In the end, players on both sides were equally to blame, and one was left with a taste of disappointment and bitterness. The game against the

Irish was won but it was desperately close. Steve Fenwick kept us in contention with his kicks and a try, before J.J. got the winning touchdown for a 20 points to 16 win. The Welsh team were exhausted; they had been cajoled during the second half by Gareth, their faces were drained, but pride and poise had motivated them sufficiently to win their Triple Triple Crown. The after-match dinner wasn't much of an event either. In the Welsh changing room one of the Welsh players singled one Irish player out by name and menacingly muttered, 'That fellow will have to come to Cardiff next year.' I realized then that matters had gone too far, the pressure and the quest for success had taken its toll, the end of this great band of Welshmen was approaching. Apart from a few oaths and profanities the Welsh changing room was a depressing scene, with quite a few of us wondering if all this, the recriminations, the sourness and the exhaustion, was worth the effort. The silence of that room spoke volumes; there really wasn't anything to celebrate. If the Irish and Welsh on that afternoon had had the opportunity of playing that game over again, I'm damned sure that it would have been more of a sporting occasion.

J.P.R., sitting on the bench socks to his ankles, was involved in his own personal analysis. He had late-tackled Mike Gibson, after Mike had kicked the ball ahead, when there was the possibility of an Irish score. They were great personal friends; the Irish had given J.P.R. a hard time throughout the match and he'd been deeply upset by all the booing. I didn't see the actual incident itself. J.P.R. said it was unintentional and a reflex action. That was good enough for me. It merely underlined how one little happening could reduce a man from being claimed as the world's greatest full-back, to that 'dirty Welsh — '. Memories are short, tempers are even shorter! There was one match to go. We needed no reminding of that fact. As we dragged ourselves off the bus taking us to the Shelbourne Hotel we were confronted by the inevitable band of Welsh supporters. The feeling of disappointment still lingered on, but up popped a red-scarved boyo and with a slap on the back declared, 'Well done, boys; now then, what about the French?'

There were fifteen men on that bus who were absolutely drained by physical exhaustion and, to a certain degree, emotional depression, and this fellow wanted to know about the French! Sometimes I think that the Welsh supporter has simply no idea of what goes on at all. Yet his question, had it been asked on the following Monday, was a legitimate one.

How on earth could we raise our game for the French? There would be a hard cup match between the Irish match and the French weekend. I honestly think that there has to be a re-examination of the international time table. Whereas the English and the Irish club players can enjoy the relatively peaceful break of a 'friendly' fixture between internationals, the Welsh players on the 'off weekends' are invariably pitched into cup ties. These are sometimes harder that the internationals and offer the body and the mind no rest at all. Add to that the Welsh squad sessions at Aberavon, Bridgend and Cardiff and there's not much adrenalin to share around them all.

Before the French match, the Afan Lido training session had gone badly and we were reduced to hoping, as do all bad actors, that everything would go right on the day. We didn't play well but the tactic of hoisting high balls for the French full-back Aguirre and allowing those two middle terriers Ray Gravell and Steve Fenwick to hound him all afternoon did the trick. Gareth was commanding as usual and I managed to score two tries, which, I was reliably informed afterwards, hadn't been done by a Welsh outside-half for forty-seven years. Who on earth keeps these records!

It was the last time that several of us appeared in a Welsh jersey, and I've no doubt that it brought nearer the beginning of the end for a few other international careers. It wasn't so much the rugby, it was the degree of concentration that was required to keep a level head in the suffocating glasshouse of Welsh rugby life. New

Faces and younger limbs were needed to take over the reins. Edwards summed it up as he entered the dressing room.

'That's it, I can't take any more.'

5

Ups and Downs

I can't remember whether I was paying the five shillings a week for a gold ring or a watch. I shall have to check with Fred the Jewellers in town. Whichever it was, it represented my unofficial engagement present to Pat Jones, the heroine of my story. I had only just reached the mature age of fifteen, and the cost of that matrimonial promise represented a major capital outlay for me. Pat was of course absolutely thrilled, my mother, when she found out, was less so. Our courtship since the beginning of schooldays had been uninterrupted; we had done all the silly things that school lovers do – met after school, sneaked out at night for walks, scribbled romantic messages on books and bits of paper – and by the age of fifteen we were both veterans of the first houses in the town's cinemas. All of this quite naturally worried both sets of parents. I can vividly recall seeing Pat's father Les driving his Wolsley car up the road to meet us; since he had publicly and vociferously declared his opposition to such a kindergarten courtship, I needed no prompting. I jumped over the wall, and used my newspaper-round knowledge of every nook and cranny in Felinfoel to get away from the irate father. We laugh about such encounters now, but I'm sure Les Jones would have half murdered me that night, if he'd caught hold of me.

My mother, as usual, was desperately worried that something would go wrong. In her own quiet way she would hint that there was something 'not nice' about two young people carrying on the way we did. I must admit, when you consider that we travelled to see Llanelli play at Maesteg, to Cardiff to see the internationals and Lynn Davies jump at Maindy stadium, we must have been crackers! Eventually my mother called in my father to sort me out, a confrontation that I assume takes place in every household when matters get a little out of hand.

'You'd better tell your father what you are doing,' she said, hoping that my father would unleash a lecture of hellfire and damnation on his wayward son. Nothing of the kind.

'Use your head, nothing bloody daft now,' he said. That was it! My mother was flabbergasted.

'Tell him!' she pleaded.

'Leave the poor kid alone.' He gave me one of those enormous winks which bind fathers and sons together, and send mothers away muttering. Pat and I were married on 21 March 1970.

Pat was carrying our child throughout the months that I was away with the 1974 Lions in South Africa. Phone calls and incessant postcards and letters kept us in contact and I knew that she was having the best of care between the two sets of parents. Pat's father, the man who would have willingly taken a birch to my backside on that lonely night years ago, was preparing our new home in Felinfoel. After my return we moved in to live with Pat's parents. It was just as well that we did so, because the next few months turned out to be a tragic and testing time for both Pat and myself.

Twenty-four hours after Stuart was born, he died. It left me numb, cold and bitter, everything in my life went out of perspective. Nothing in the world mattered – the tours, the jerseys, the tries were totally insignificant. I withdrew into a shell. I remember travelling to Swansea to sign some kind of death certificate and I remember holding that small box of a coffin before the funeral. All attempts at rationalizing what had happened failed. I just walked around in a stupor, looking for something or someone to blame. I thought how selfish I had been, travelling thousands of miles away when my rightful place should have been with Pat. She was anxious to get out of hospital, and, as soon as she was discharged we went on our first and only real holiday since we've been married.

The last thing in my mind was rugby and I decided to give up the sport. Week after week went by without any interest being shown, though to their eternal credit the boys at Llanelli kept pestering me to come out and give it a go. At first it was useless, but a few weeks later I decided to give in and went with Llanelli to Northampton. The enthusiasm wasn't there, however, and I returned home hating the game and everything to do with it. I still don't know what changed my mind; perhaps it was the continual encouragement of family, friends and colleagues. I know that Pat wanted me to carry on, and the doctor's edict had certainly perked me up a little. 'Get her pregnant as quickly as you can,' was the command. I did, and Steven was born on 26 November 1975

There is no doubt that such experiences challenge the essence of one's existence. It brought us both together, and I was given a better perspective on life. I was determined that rugby would never again dominate my entire being; there were more important things to achieve and appreciate. But I will have to admit that the game also became a crutch to lean on in the later years.

Ironically Steven's birth led to a series of domestic dramas that gave the Welsh rugby media their best story of the 1975 season. The tale has been immortalized by that jovial minstrel from Glynneath, Max Boyce, and the full text would give him a modern opera.

I had been determined to shake off the memories of the previous season and had spent some time during the summer with Carmarthen Harriers, working on my speed. I felt as fit as I had ever done before a season and, since the Australians had to be met in the first few months, that was no bad thing.

Steven was born on a Wednesday, and on the Saturday Pat was released from Morriston Hospital. I picked her up with our new welcome addition, but no sooner had we started on our journey home, when we were flagged down by the Llanelli RFC bus on its way to Senghenydd to play in a cup match. They were desperately short and pleaded with me to play. Considering what had happened to Pat before, there was no way I was going to miss the homecoming! If nothing else, the Llanelli committee are doggedly obstinate; they wouldn't give up and eventually, after returning home, much to my in-laws' annoyance I turned the car towards Senghenydd, not having a clue where it was. Fate struck again; I was injured in the match, and had to phone John Dawes the Welsh coach and tell him about my injured foot.

'We'll see about it on Thursday at the run-out.' But at Waterton Cross the pain was too much and the next twenty-four hours convinced me that I wasn't fit. I phoned John again, told him that I couldn't kick, so my use to the Welsh team was negligible, and dropped out of the Australian game. It so happened that, on the Monday evening, Llanelli had a game against Bath at Stradey Park and I made myself available, having agreed with Bernard Thomas on the dubious tactic that he would do all the kicking and I would merely act as a 'passenger' and passer of the ball. I didn't kick all evening, but my presence in that Llanelli team was noticed by the Welsh selectors. It wasn't appreciated.

Later that season I was picked to play in the final trial. It heartens me to find that, at last, the Welsh selectors have accepted that the trials are a farce; hardly anyone wants to play in them and they are no more of an indication of how a national fifteen are going to play on the day than a video recording of any previous international. It's not surprising that Wales suffers a chronic attack of influenza around trial time; I have yet to see the two sides line up against each other as selected. I didn't play in that particular final trial (flu!) and again my absence was noted. Wales was due to play against England in a fortnight's time.

The phone rang on the Saturday night of the trial and Peter Jackson of the *Daily Mail* asked me if I'd heard the names of the Welsh squad. I hadn't. Peter then informed me that I was out of the squad and asked me for my reaction. I can't even remember what I told him, because I resented the fact that a member of the press was privy to the knowledge before I was. In no way did I hold it against Peter Jackson for phoning me up – that was his job – but I have never understood why a member of the Big Five didn't have the common courtesy to give me a ring to explain why I had been dropped. Some would argue that such a procedure isn't warranted. To those I would say that politeness costs very little and would save a great deal of personal torment. Others have suffered in the same way: Gerald was dropped from the Welsh team without explanation; Ray Gravell heard about his omission from the Welsh team on a car radio. It is about time that we thought drastically about the way we treat our players, not only at national level but at club level as well.

The next seven days were bewildering. There was a national protest. 'BENNETT OUT OF SQUAD', 'BENNETT NUMBER THREE!', 'BRITISH LION DEMOTED'. I remember travelling in the car listening to a phone-in on Swansea Sound, the local commercial radio station, and a Mrs Jones complaining to the DJ 'I think it's terrible what they've done to that lovely little boy from Felinfoel!' If any of the Welsh selectors had ventured into Llanelli after the squad announcement, I think a host of people would have seen to it that they would have left via the Loughor river. For my own part I was naturally disappointed and annoyed but had decided that I would send a telegram of good wishes to John Bevan on the morning of the match. I had no doubt that my withdrawal from the Australian match and the final trial had caused my relegation. I was being given six of the best – in public.

On the Saturday, I played for Llanelli and we had decided to go on a family outing on the Sunday. Indeed, it was a rare pleasure to be home at the weekend. The phone rang and we were in two minds whether to answer it, since in all probability it was one of those 'you'll get back in, don't worry Phil' calls. It wasn't, it was Handel Rogers, who apart from being a member of the Llanelli club was also the WRU President. What on earth did he want? The car was ready to go and Pat and Steve were in it.

'Can you come down to the training session at Aberavon. You're in the team for Saturday against England. John Bevan had pulled out and David Richards has pulled a hamstring.'

Why had they delegated Handel to phone me – he wasn't one of the selectors? Not one of the so-called Big Five had had the courage to phone. Their reticent behaviour at Aberavon was even worse.

A few of the boys were laughing as I had expected them to do. John Bevan, who had originally been chosen, called me a 'jammy bugger' and I indeed felt genuinely sorry for him. But the selectors couldn't look me in the eye. 'Clive Rowlands did come down to see you to explain, didn't he?' said one of them, knowing full well that no one had been anywhere near Llanelli. Even Clive acknowledged that Llanelli hadn't been on his itinerary during the past seven days. 'I took so much abuse on the phone, I couldn't take any more. So I said to hell with it!' Telephones were obviously a scarce commodity in Upper Cwmtwrch.

John Dawes was by far the most embarrassed and offered quite easily the worst excuse. 'We knew you wouldn't like subbing and we knew you wouldn't relish the prospect of sitting on the bench against England.'

I had never heard such utter tripe in all my life. It had all the ingredients of a Welsh Watergate cover-up. My answer to them came on the field when Wales took the Grand Slam and I broke the Welsh points record.

Perhaps some may think I am a little harsh, but there were further instances which soured my respect for the administration of the Welsh Rugby Union and its servants. I should stress that people whom I have admired for a long time are associated with the day-to-day running of the game in Wales, and I will continue to admire them. I feel at times, though, that there are some who appoint themselves as demi-gods, who care not for the well-being of the most important people in rugby, the players, but only for the continuing preservation of their own prestige and importance. These are the spokesmen who insist that the game of rugby football is still amateur but are the first to insist on professional results. The honour of playing for Wales, I know, should be sufficient in itself, and, as players, I suppose we should never expect any understanding or consideration from the bureaucratic powers that be, the 'alikadoos' as they are often called in the changing rooms. Others are talked of in less affectionate terms.

I didn't speak to the late Gordon Rowley for three years after our particular 'tiff'. Llanelli had been drawn to play against Crynant in the WRU Cup and an annoying back injury which had troubled me for some time suddenly became a persistent aggravation. It forced me to pull out of the cup and I decided to do something about the injury. I'd had some cortisone injections before but the discomfort seemed to increase with every game. Llanelli decided to make an appointment with the WRU surgeon, Gordon Rowley, at Swansea Hospital. Three doctors examined me and they suggested that I return to Morriston Hospital on the following day.

Rowley told me that I would have to miss a bit of rugby, but wasn't so sure how long it would be. The first corrective measure for what he diagnosed as a spinal deficiency was to place me in a jacket. He explained what the spine trouble was in medical mumbo-jumbo. The examination took place in his office, with all manner of pins being stuck in my back. He left the office and, in a

75

corridor full of people curious to see and find out why I was there, he told Pat, who'd come along with me, 'I'm afraid your husband will never play rugby again. If he does he'll end up as a cripple.'

Pat told me about this conversation as soon as we'd got into the car. I was staggered. It was a crushing blow and you can imagine my anger when the local *Western Mail* reporter knocked on our door half an hour after our return from Morriston. I know for a fact that neither Pat nor myself had spoken to anyone.

The rage I felt against Rowley's handling of the affair quickly disappeared when the thought struck me that he could be right and I was placing myself in danger if I walked onto a rugby pitch again. I had to get a second opinion from somewhere and I met up with Dickie Rees, a doctor at Glangwili hospital, a man who, together with the staff of the Carmarthen hospital, has become essential to the welfare of the Bennett family. As ever, the Glangwili people were kind and, thank goodness, a little more reassuring. 'Yes,' said Dickie, 'you've got a spinal deficiency, but so have thousands of others and they don't even know about it.'

There was a glimmer of hope ... and that ingredient will always keep the optimist's flame alight. I travelled to Liverpool to see another specialist, Professor Roth, a charming gentleman who gave me a thorough examination, asking me to do all kinds of exercises in his examination room. It was here that I also came across Maldwyn Griffiths, another doctor, who a few years later I was to meet again with Dickie Rees, for a knee operation. I think those two could keep the *Lancet* going with articles simply by confining themselves to the quirks of the Bennett physique. However, at this time, Professor Roth's conclusions on the back injury were music to my ears.

'The deficiency is there, but it shouldn't stop you from playing.' I could have kissed him. But I'm a bit of a worrier and just in case the news from Liverpool might be bad I had set up another appointment in Shrewsbury with Dennis Brookes, an osteopath whose reputation for instant and miraculous cures had been widely publicized. I was rather elated when I arrived there with Professor Roth's diagnosis, but my mood changed as soon as I saw Mr Brookes's waiting room. There were people there with all kinds of deformities and handicaps. It was a particularly depressing sight and I felt that I had no real need to be there at all. However, I was eventually seen, and was given a form of treatment that I can only describe as strange, but the ride home was filled with visions of the waiting room and an over-riding feeling of gratitude that I had only a minor back injury to think about.

Whether Gordon Rowley was right or wrong in his diagnosis is not my privilege to question. What I do question is his right to tell Pat that my rugby was finished in a crowded corridor with a hundred eyes and ears about. There's nothing we like more in Wales than sympathizing with the sick. I have since comforted myself knowing that in the late Mr Rowley's 'he'll never play again' ward, I would have had the company of England cricketer Tony Lewis, Gerald Davies and Allan Martin. An England captain and two Lions!

Eventually, my feelings towards Rowley simmered down a little. Through the years we became a little closer and whatever I may have thought at that time was forgotten with the realization that he, too, thought that he was doing his best for us.

There are compensations in international rugby, and fortunately there have been so many that I hope the years will erase the bitterness of a few isolated incidents. No one can imagine the pleasure that rugby has given me over the years, the opportunities that have come my way. I can only hope with all the will in the world to repay some of my debts. One such highlight was the OBE presentation. It was great excitement: the hire of the suit, the buying of new dresses for my mother and Pat, wondering what the Queen would ask. I can be as cool as a cucumber in front of 50,000 Welshmen, but the thought of meeting Her Royal Highness on her home ground petrified me. I don't remember who sent the letter, I think it was signed by the Prime Minister, but there it stood on the mantelpiece for days, just in case somebody popped in to doubt that I'd had it.

It's funny how personal such invitations seem until you arrive at Buckingham Palace to find out that the postman has been delivering hundreds of similar letters all around the country. We spotted the Two Ronnies, who were being honoured as well, but the only other person that we could identify was the Queen herself. It's quite unnerving waiting in that long line before the introduction, not knowing exactly what to do with your hands. You can't exactly put them in your pocket can you? It was all over too quickly, but it took some time to climb down from the elation of meeting 'Maam'. I realize that the award was a tribute to the efforts of the Lions in New Zealand, but I did get a huge personal kick out of it. In the Bennett household anything can happen and, months later, I found the immaculately inscribed parchment in a box, suitably endorsed by four-year-old Stephen's crayons!

The royal connection didn't end there, since Pat and myself were invited to sit in the Number 1 box at Wimbledon during the summer. Both of us are tennis fanatics and we needed no second bidding when the invitations came. It was quite hilarious joining the traffic outside the All England headquarters and being guided towards the Royal car park with the Daimlers, Rolls Royces and limousines – and us sitting in my freshly cleaned Cortina. The attendant gave us a right going-over, but couldn't dispute the authenticity of our tickets. The chairman of the Sports Council and former England scrum-half Dickie Jeeps was there, which helped a great deal. He was used to this type of treatment and he also knew the difference between Indian and China tea! These are moments that I shall savour – the doors that opened up which otherwise would have been beyond the contemplation of Phil Bennett, CP school.

I've also been allowed a brief insight into the world of soccer. The brief flirtation that I had with professional soccer has only served to intensify my admiration for the game. It was always difficult to explain to people, especially Welsh selectors, that I preferred watching Swansea City at the Vetch Field to being a spectator at Stradey. As a player there was far too much involvement in the game to be a passive spectator, but hopefully now I shall become a reformed character and sit quietly and attentively in the stand.

I can recall being asked whether I was available and then totally ignored by the selectors who were picking a fifteen to play against New Zealand, simply because I'd gone to the Vetch on the Saturday before selection, rather than sit in the stand watching the Scarlets. The involvement at Stradey is too great, sitting there fretting and frustrating over mistakes done by Llanelli, watching their every move and feeling totally depressed if things go wrong. Over the years I've kept my close association with a number of Swansea City people and the management there have always opened their doors for rugby people needing treatment for specialized sporting injuries. It's the same for a number of rugby players. Gareth (the Edwards hamstring again) knows the physio room at the Vetch as well as John Toshack; more recently both Gareth Davies and Terry Holmes have become Ninian Park regulars.

But, if I feel at home at the Vetch either receiving treatment or watching from the terraces, my first soccer love has always been, and always will be, Manchester United. Theirs is the result that I've always looked for first on a Saturday night. It all stems back, I suppose, to the tragic Munich air disaster where so many of the talented United team perished. Ever since then, they have been my idols; even that man Denis Law, who once wore the United jersey, was never forgiven in the Bennett household when, wearing a Manchester City shirt, he

79

scored to put United in the second division. When the Welsh team were in Argentina in 1968, United were also there, but for reasons which were beyond my comprehension – something about security – we weren't allowed to go and see them.

Possibly one of the saddest sporting spectacles was during the 1974 Lions tour to South Africa when Gareth and myself managed to get tickets to go and see a soccer match between the Jewish Guild and Cape Town. George Best and the 1966 World Cup skipper Bobby Moore were playing, but unfortunately the excitement of going to the match quickly turned sour. It was as if Best didn't care about the game ... or his pride. Yet there were thousands of people who had turned up to watch and possibly witness one piece of Best magic. It seemed that this genius of a footballer was simply content to stand in the middle, take only a moderate interest in the game and disappoint all those people, who would have been satisfied with only one example of his multiple talents. I had seen George Best before in his prime, waltzing past defenders with changes of speed and the ball 'tied' to his boots – and I wanted these people to experience the same thrill. Sadly, the portly Best showed no pride in his professionalism. Nevertheless even that image-shattering experience hasn't been enough to diminish my fanaticism for United.

My support for the soccer stars wasn't totally exclusive to United though. Any team with a Welshman playing for them, especially one in the First Division, automatically interested me. I followed Toshack at Liverpool, Terry Yorath at Leeds, Leighton James at Burnley and Mike England at Spurs. I know for a fact too, that they in turn followed the exploits of the Welsh rugby team with equal fanaticism. Trevor Francis has become something of a rugby devotee. It helped when he married a Llanelli girl ... ever since then he's been bitten by the bug. During his long injury he became quite a frequent visitor to Stradey Park, and there is one story about Trevor which he loves to tell himself. He had come to the Reddings to see the Sam Doble memorial match and after the game one of the fans walked up to him and asked for his autograph. Trevor willingly obliged, but was somewhat taken aback when the autograph hunter expressed disappointment, having thought he'd captured Andy Irvine's signature!

There seems to be close affinity between sportsmen who have achived recognition for their abilities in their respective spheres. I've no doubt that the fraternity is nurtured by admiration for its members' gifts. I remember asking Barry John after he'd appeared on the BBC television programme 'A Question of Sport' what kind of people his co-competitors had been. 'What's Francis Lee like?'

'All right,' said the Cefneithin wonder, who is as fast with his tongue as he was on the field. 'He was the number one centre-forward in the country, and I was the number one outside-half ... I didn't worry about him.' My two colleagues on that same programme were Lou Macari of Manchester United and England cricketer Derek Randall. I had just watched Randall score 170 in a centenary test match, and was about to approach him and congratulate him on his feat when he asked me for my autograph!

That particular interlude of intersport comradeship was enjoyable. No less enjoyable but far more exacting was my introduction to the Superstars competition held at Cwmbran. Weighing in at twelve stone ten, and after a heavy night at a dinner function where I was awarded the Swansea Sportsman of the Year trophy, I was not in ideal condition for any kind of activity, let alone a 7 a.m. 50-metre swim. In fact, after a surfeit of celebrations I was in no shape at all. Gareth, who had already competed before in a blaze of publicity, gave me the soundest advice possible – 'Enjoy it.' I tried desperately hard to remember his words of wisdom as I dived into the swimming pool knowing that some of the others were already approaching the other end.

The contest gave me the opportunity of getting to

know Duncan McKenzie as we vied against the likes of Andy Irvine (fit as ever), judo champion Brian Jacks (who had trained for the event for months) and water skier Mike Hazlewood (who had gone into hibernation in an Army camp). A Former Superstars competition was being run in conjunction with our own event with Bobby Charlton, John Charles, Brian Close and Olympic swimming competitors Ian Black and Brian Phelps sweating it out, in what appeared to be a far more entertaining sequence.

Brian Jacks had committed himself solely to the purpose of winning all that was at stake. There was nothing wrong in that, but his single-minded approach hadn't gone unnoticed by the 'elder' sportsmen. Brian had brought with him to Cwmbran his parents, wife, coach and physio, and at the end of the two days the 'Gentle Giant' John Charles strolled up to him. 'How much have you won, Brian?'

'Fifteen hundred quid,' came the reply.

'Just as well,' said John. 'You'll need that to pay the hotel bill for that lot.'

6

South Africa

'Having a good time, weather fine, and I hope we win the series.' I must have sent over 500 cards to friends at home conveying the same sentiments, secretly hoping that Mrs Evans and Mr Jones back home wouldn't compare notes on how Phil was doing in South Africa. My reputation as a prolific postcard-writer was I suppose well deserved, and to my inquisitive colleagues on tour who could never work out what on earth I could find to say to all those people, I have now exposed my linguistic lack of originality.

I've never been a comfortable tourist and the cards, the letters, and the phone calls to Pat – usually inspired by heady celebrations – have always kept my yearning for the home patch at arm's length – except perhaps in New Zealand in 1977. South Africa in 1974 was different. We were winning.

It was one glorious achievement. As each challenge was swept aside as we moved from the lowlands to the high veldt, the Lions of Willie John McBride generated a quality that is rarely achieved by British teams – confidence. No matter how a team goes about gaining that quality, whether it be by dedication, determination, skill or coaching, it is essential to possess it, especially on tour. Time passes quickly for a successful touring party, and I know full well that three months away from home when things are not going well can turn out to be an eternal nightmare. The Lions of 1974 had all the qualities that I've mentioned before ... and they also had Willie John and Syd Millar on board.

From that very first match against Western Transvaal when Willie John, delighted to get the first victory underneath his belt, announced, 'The show is on the road,' to the end of the fourth test party when he declared 'It's been great travelling with you men,' he was a leader of great courage and inspiration. He had a memorable quip for every occasion; he had the tolerance and patience to lend an ear of to any of his men's grievances or worries. Above all, he had everyone's respect. That the four home unions had chosen the complementary pair from Ballymena, McBride and Syd Millar, showed considerable foresight. Both were committed to winning in South Africa, a commitment, I suspect, born out of the frustration of being there in 1966 and losing the test series three–nil.

Willie John was a mature captain and, with the tour going well, it was always comforting to see that contented look on his face. He valued his players and the compliment was returned. 'No prisoners will be taken' was one of the Ballymena catch phrases. Also, though he had sufficient experience to dwarf the inhibitions of a newcomer to a Lions jersey, his advice was always tempered with humour. Such was the degree of respect for the big man that, when we faced the second test match against the Springboks, he had only to ask of us to win it for him and the response was immediate.

Syd Millar, who probably realized that there was sufficient guile and knowledge entrusted in his captain, remained a little aloof from the players. This was no bad thing and I intend it as a compliment to his qualities of understanding. A hard player in his time, he was a man who commanded our respect. His analysis of the game and of every situation was thorough, and the attention given to the players' welfare almost motherly. One would hear him often in the early hours of the morning summon a waiter to bring twenty steak sandwiches and a crate of beer – merely because one of the company had complained of slight peckishness. His philosophy was simple but effective: if the players gave of their best on the field, they deserved nothing but the best off it. Mind you, on the practice field he could murder us.

On returning home, people would ask, 'How on earth did you win the series?' I honestly believe that the success achieved against the Springboks was based on the training-fields of Stilfontein. We had arrived there nine days before our first match. By the end of our time, some of the forwards were nearly reduced to tears, several bore the scars and blisters of almost continuous scrummaging practice ... but eventually Syd had moulded a forward combination that was not only going to surprise the South African public but take their much-prized packs apart as well.

Somehow, because of the common determination all these individuals blended together into the most successful British Lions team ever. I think that Gareth surpassed his previous achievements on the field and added another facet to the Gwauncaegurwen armoury, that of positive attitude. It is no state secret that he wasn't the best of trainers but in South Africa, possibly because of his admiration for Willie John, Gareth became a far more mature player. An injury to John Maloney, the other scrum-half, forced the management to play Gareth in a long tortuous series of games, despite the fact that he was injured himself. He knew that if he came off the field in the third test the Lions would be forced to play flanker Tony Neary at scrum-half. And what a friend and partner Gareth is, both on and off the field.

Edwards, ever since he produced a Welsh-language single record, is convinced that he is something of a Sir Geraint Evans. I would be the last to hurt his vanity by suggesting that he has a bad voice, but there are times to appreciate the vocal cords and there are times when such noises irritate and puncture the limits of tolerance. On the eve of the game against Transvaal, 'G.O.' was to be heard singing at the top of his voice from his hotel balcony. Despite all protests, both friendly and alien, there was no stopping him and the impromptu performance carried on without any sign of a respite. It so happened that I was rooming with Dick Milliken directly above Gareth. The nerves had suffered enough so there was nothing left to do but send a paper bucket full of water over the balcony. It was a direct hit!

He was furious and bounded up the stairs, banging on every door and threatening whoever was responsible with dire consequences. But there's one thing about Gareth, he's persistent ... and it wasn't long before he was out on the balcony once again, wooing the passers-by with yet another Celtic melody. Down went another bucket and again the artillery found its target. The stairs were cleared five at a time, he ripped Mike Burton's shirt passing him on the stairs, and shook every door on our corridor until the hinges were loose in a vain attempt to discover the phantom bucket-thrower. I honestly believe that he would have done me a permanent injury had he found out it was me. So, with that in mind, I only found the courage to own up to the deed several years after-wards, before a Welsh game, and even then I suspect that behind the little laugh there still lingered a huge reserve of hostility.

Yet here was the man who saved my bacon on more than one occasion. After the win in the first test, Willie John had declared, 'It's Saturday night, victory has been achieved and I take no responsibility until Monday morning.' I should have been wiser and taken his advice and limited the celebrations. The party went on for days. On the Monday evening Gareth and I together with J.J. and Bobby Windsor were invited out to a family cele-bration. It was a night out too good to miss and I knew that I hadn't been picked for the following day's game against the Universities. Syd always arranged a meeting of the players on the evening before match days, but Edwards reassured me that we would get back to the hotel in time. Beer after beer was sunk at our host's home and, but for the solicitous attitude of Gareth, I'm sure we would have missed the talk. On our way back to the hotel, after reassuring our hosts that we would return,

Gareth stressed that I shouldn't take part in any way in the team discussion lest I should give the game away. But it was too much of a temptation.

Staggering to my feet, I mumbled something inaudible. Before Syd could ask me for clarification, Edwards grabbed the back of my sweater and unceremoniously dumped me back in the chair. We returned to the party.

The next morning was one I would like to forget, for at eleven a.m. Syd Millar walked into the room and announced that the team had been changed and I had to play. I thought, and offered every medical excuse in the book but there was no convincing the Irishman, and I simply couldn't wriggle out. The actual game is also best forgotten, but what I do remember was asking the referee to blow up early. Neither the mud not the exercise managed to get rid of my hangover.

There were other players on tour who gave the party a *camaraderie* of humour and good nature. I became especially friendly with 'The Duke', Pontypool's hooker Bobby Windsor. Bobby made his mark on the tour before we had even set foot on South African soil. He is the world's worst air traveller and, though I sympathize with the torment that any apprehensive airborne passenger must go through, I have to admit that, looking back, Bobby's performance on the plane to South Africa had its humorous moments. J.P.R. didn't help matters either. The Duke was groaning in agony and feeling violently sick on the way over, so he went to seek the advice of 'The Doctor'. J.P.R., who was trying to sleep off the effects of a round of GTs, suggested that Bobby partake of the same. The diagnosis wasn't well received and left the invalid to question whether J.P.R. had passed any medical examinations at all. When we eventually arrived his condition had worsened and we were all quite alarmed. But, as he was carted away on a stretcher towards the awaiting ambulance, he could be heard for miles around warning any would-be-doctor-cum-butcher that had any thoughts of putting a knife to his body exactly what the consequences would be. No one, as it happened, was required to give Bobby any kind of surgical treatment and he rejoined us at Stilfontein after a few days of convalescence in hospital.

The sheer boredom of Stilfontein, which can compare only with being stuck on a wet Saturday night at Maesteg's bus station waiting for the last service to Bridgend, was again relieved by the Windsor wit. The choice of this small town as our first headquarters was an excellent one from the coaching point of view. There was little to distract the players from the task at hand. But the team's hotel had a parrot, a very loquacious bird at that. Several of us wondered at Bobby's fascination for the bird, as he could be seen sitting with it for hours on end. The puzzle was finally resolved when our feathered friend could be heard letting loose a torrent of abusive words to hotel guests and staff. The poor bird had been ruined for life!

As a matter of policy each player was allocated a different room-mate at frequent intervals. There were those who were tidy and quiet, there were some who took great pleasure in reading or playing cards, but it was always the unpredictable ones that fascinated me. Andy Ripley was the most unpredictable of the lot, and the one man responsible for sending manager Alun Thomas's hair greyer than it already was. Often you would enter a room to find 'Rippers' in some kind of transcendental meditation with the incense paper burning away and the England number eight lost to the world. He hardly had any luggage, finding that two plastic carrier bags were sufficient to carry his worldly possessions; no matter how important the reception, the Rippers' attire would normally consist of a blazer, tie, no shirt, jeans and flip-flops. No one really minded – the well-being of the party had to allow for that kind of non-conformity.

The other non-conformist was Mickey Burton, who could be found holding court with the press at regular intervals. He had even less luggage than Andy. One suitcase, one spare shirt, a pair of socks and one clean set of underwear. Every single member of the team that

shared with Mickey was resigned to keeping him supplied with toothpaste, shaving cream; and Lord help you
if you were one to indulge in 'smellies' – aftershave,
deodorant and that sort of thing. But both he and the
other oddities, and I use that word advisedly, had one
factor in common: they took great pride in playing for the
Lions and never shirked their responsibilities. It was
good to have them on tour.

Another uniting force in South Africa was the constant
banter of the next challenge. After each victory the
clarion call of the following fixture would be sounded.
'Wait till you get to Western Province,' the locals would
shout. 'The Quaggas will give you a hiding.' 'You'll
never beat us on the High Veldt.' The South Africans
were somewhat incensed by our winning ways and
panicked into incredible selection errors, believing that
our good fortune was merely bad fortune on their part.
Sometimes the jibing taunts got the better of our
humour. I can remember walking into a bar with Bobby
Windsor when an Italian waiter who knew as much
about rugby as Bobby knew about spaghetti began a
familiar jibe. 'You guys will never win the test series,' he
chortled, looking around for support form the other
customers. Under normal circumstances the statement
would either have been ignored or acknowledged with a
chuckle. However, that afternoon Bobby had lost a few
'heads,' which was tantamount to his virility being
questioned, and I had played a poor game; all we wanted
to do was enjoy a few beers and indulge in a self-pitying
session. The Italian, however, would not let go and was
annoyingly persistent. In no time at all Bobby left the
table, shuffled over to our friend, seized him by his coat,
raised his body a few feet off the ground and up against
the wall and let loose a few oaths that not even the parrot
at Stilfontein would have repeated. A hell of a man to
have in your corner is The Duke.

Despite the success of the 1974 Lions I have to admit
that it could so easily have been different for me personally. Often one finds that luck or fate plays a major part

in a career. The injury to Alan Old in the disgraceful
game against the Proteas cost him his moment of glory,
since Alan at that time was the favourite to wear the
number ten jersey in the test series. His kicking was on
song and I'd had that poor game against Western
Province. I felt genuinely sorry for him, whilst the late
and illegal tackling in that game deepened our resolve to
conquer the Springboks. One of the most moving
moments on that tour was the visit of the entire touring
team to Alan's hospital bed after the first test match and
the sight of the likeable fellow smiling but recognizing
that the tour was over for him made me quite teary-eyed.

His painful trip from the field to the hospital was quite
an event. He'd been felled by a questionable tackle and
was writhing in pain on the ground; Syd Millar asked me
to accompany him to hospital. The vehicle driver had
obviously been brought up on tales of the Keystone
Cops: goodness knows how many bollards he knocked
over trying to get out of the ground ... and then it took
him an endless amount of time to find the gate.
Meanwhile Alan, now suffering a quite considerable
degree of pain, was being thrown from one side of the
vehicle to the other despite the attention of what seemed
to be a forty-stone-plus nurse. Once on the road the
antics of the driver quietened down a bit; then after
arriving at the hospital, somehow he and I had to
negotiate a forty-step flight of stairs with Alan complaining of increasing pain. The nurse had her own problems
tackling the stairs, the look on her face suggesting that
she had volunteered for her last game of rugby duty.
Once we'd conquered the ascent we discovered that our
Vasco da Gama of an ambulance driver had taken us to
an old people's home and the whole process of clamber-
ing poor old Alan to hospital had to start all over again.
Yet throughout the ordeal I had nothing but admiration
for Alan's courage and the philosophical way that he
outwardly responded to his injury. Not once did he vent
any bitterness.

The companionship was good and the morale was

high. In contrast, the attitude and mood of the South Africa camp was one of grave seriousness. Their hospitality during that tour and during subsequent visits to South Africa was of the highest order. The visits to their homes and the warmth of the welcome at times lulls the tourists into a false sense of security. Our liaison officer, and indeed the 'Nanny' of several tours, was an incredible man. Choet Visser must have more friends across the world than any man alive – indeed his own private rugby museum testifies to the high esteem that Lions, All Blacks, Australians and Argentinians have for him. Nothing was too much trouble for Choet; it's been said with some justification that his presence has been far more conducive to the well-being of touring players than many a management team. The South Africans, though, dearly love to win. I would like to put it a little more strongly than that. The Welshman hates defeat, but the little sporting activity that South Africa is allowed to indulge in makes it that much more imperative for them to win. If anything, this is detrimental to their attitude towards sport, the pressure on the young South African being enormous. However, here we had a touring team that had questioned the superiority of South African scrummaging, once their forte, and such was the power of the Lions that for a while nothing else in the country mattered. We became front-page news. The South Africans' natural determination to win hardly allows them to enjoy the game, or so it seems to me. After their first defeat in the test series we were told that the Springboks had been taken away to a retreat where papers and radio reports about the Lions were banned. I find all that unnecessary: it only leads to an unhealthy atmosphere on the field where frustration becomes manifest in short tempers. Yet such is the pressure on the South African to win.

By the time that the first test took place we were well aware of what to expect. However, on that day the foundation of good scrummaging and close support play as preached by Syd found the Lions pack getting on top, and behind them Gareth was at his rascal best – he even dropped a goal.

I felt an immense amount of pride coming off that field in a British Lions jersey. It was a good feeling which generated confidence that we could hold our heads up high until the next encounter with the Springboks. Yet I knew that in the stand and at home there were other outside-halves who could have done the job that afternoon. When it comes to selection, there is an immense amount of luck in being in the right place at the right time. Walking off that field I could remember that strange nervousness driving the car on Gower and hoping to hear the composition of the Lions team on the radio. I'd pulled the car into a lay-by and had prepared myself for disappointment. There even seemed to me a hesitancy in the announcer's voice when the names of the half-backs were announced. Yet, here I was after a test win, thousands of miles from home, full of pride since I had now played for the British Lions. It was an overwhelming emotional moment ... and what's more we had won by 12 points to 3.

The South African press weren't convinced, and predicted our downfall in the next test, as we moved to higher ground and Pretoria. In the meantime a half-fit, flu-affected Lions team, had beaten Transvaal, one of the strongest of the provincial teams, albeit narrowly. We'd also been to Rhodesia, which to all intents and purposes was time we used to gather adrenalin for the second test.

Though I had what I considered to be my best match for the Lions in the second test, it nearly cost me the tour. McCullen clipped my leg as I was going to the line and the pain was severe. The doctor and J.P.R. had misgivings about my continuing on the field of play, but an appeal from Willie John persuaded me that, despite the rather ominous rush of blood from my foot, going off would have solved little. We won the game 28 to 9, and we knew that the series was ours if injuries and overconfidence escaped us. On the latter score there was no problem. Syd Millar would see to that.

The celebrations after the second test were quite magnificent. We had all been taken to Kruger Park and billeted out in huts quite near to the animal-reserve fences. Mervyn Davies, who was enjoying some considerable pleasure both on and off the field during the tour, was in charge of 'Sunday School', a euphemism for a letting-of-the-hair-down drinking session. Wine, steaks and the Zambezi river combined to make it a memorable afternoon, and after a quiet cat-nap I went down for dinner. Other members of the party, the more resilient ones, carried on with the festivities, and by this time some were being carried out too! Enter Merv the Swerv, unshaven – ''cause it'll make me look meaner on the field' – cigarette in mouth and carrying two crates of beer on his shoulders. The session continued until we all heard an almighty crash in one of the huts or rondavels as they were called.

Willie John picked me up as we went to investigate. The sight was incredible. Inside one of the rondavels there sat Ian McLauchlan with a blanket around his shoulders, and some six inches of beer swirling around his ankles. Billy Steele of Scotland had made a vain attempt to drink J.P.R. under the table and was never the same on tour again – and Mervyn was still sober enough to orchestrate the fiasco.

Again Willie John, a veteran of such parties, decided that a retreat was called for. Picking me up again he went into the pitch-black darkness of the night in search of a bed. Fortunately we heard Merv rally the troops inside, who were bent on doing something mischievous to my room.

'I think we'd better go and look for my hut,' said the big man. There I was on his back, because of my stitches, as we tried to look for the numbers on the outside of the buildings. It was all pretty hopeless and suddenly we found ourselves leaning up against the reserve fences.

A lion growled and for the life of me I've never seen a second-row man react so quickly. He picked me up and went haring across the ground. Suddenly everything went blank as my head hit a low branch. Such was Willie John's preoccupation in getting away from the beast that he hardly noticed that I was no longer his passenger ... until a desperate cry for help brought him back. Eventually, after a search, the bed was found; there was much amusement in the party when Willie John and I were discovered in bed next morning, fully clothed, and myself sporting a large lump on my forehead.

The Springbok selectors after the defeats of the first and second tests were thrown into some confusion. This was prompted, I feel, by the shock of their assumed invincibility being penetrated by a far better forward unit than they'd anticipated. We suddenly became accepted by the cynics of the South African press and the Thomasesque characters of our own media party – notably John Reason. There were ugly encounters, however, with the South African public. The will to beat us became a national obsession, though for some sectors of the society, for instance my adopted and faithful supporters at Durban High School, there were unforgettable moments of genuine friendship.

The games leading up to, and after, the third test were bad-tempered and predictably controversial. Willie John nearly took the whole team off the field against Natal after J.P.R. had unwisely lost his cool after tackling the local hero Tommy Bedford ... the referee was pelted and assaulted after our match against the Quaggas ... and in our match against the Orange Free State the refereeing was quite the most dreadful I'd ever encountered. Added to this, both sets of news reporters had turned fiction-writers and were to be complimented on their imaginative stories of naked women in corridors and all-night drinking revelries. Again, all this was counterproductive for the Springboks. It just made us more determined.

If there was one game that should have provided conclusive evidence that the 1974 Lions team had achieved a level of distinction unsurpassed by previous Lions teams in South Africa, it was the third test. After my injury sustained against the Boks in the second international, I had tried out my ankle against the Bantu team and, with the help of four painkilling injections, was declared fit to play for the test. Again the South African selectors, confused and concerned, selected a Springboks side which showed eleven changes from the game at Pretoria, delaying the choice of scrum-half until the morning of the match. The Lions were dominant throughout; Andy Irvine kicked two penalties, one from inside his own half, and he converted one of the three tries that were scored (one by Gordon Brown and two by J.J. Williams). The series had been won and our line in the test matches hadn't been crossed. On the way back to the changing room Willie John saluted the reserves in the stand ... victory had been achieved and he knew more than anyone that without the support and commitment of the 'Wednesdays', sitting in the stand – the Ralstons and the Burtons – the smile on his face wouldn't have been so wholesome.

Yet again, we were to run into trouble from the South African press. J.P.R. more than anyone suffered unduly as a result of the 'Bedford incident', while the rest of us were amused, but sometimes angered, by fictitious stories of bawdy nights and drunken lechery. They were nowhere near the mark, but it showed the desperate desire in some South African quarters to discredit us. Our hosts the genuine supporters, though sad and perplexed, were as generous as ever.

Inevitably our concentration waned somewhat before the last and final hurdle of the series. The very last test match produced an incident that I would willingly like to erase from the memory banks. There were three controversial tries in the match refereed by Max Baise who had been in charge of the first test. There was the suggestion that Roger Uttley had not grounded the ball properly for the first Lions try, while a try by South African Peter Cronje was adjudged by most of us to have been the result of a knock-on. Be that as it may, the South Africans had tied the game up at 13 points all when the Lions went after their line with a vengeance, with seconds remaining on the clock. The 75,000 crowd were frantic with excitement and the Lions were dog-tired, but here was the last inspired move. J.P.R. came into the line, found Fergus Slattery outside him, and there is no doubt in my mind that the Irishman did ground the ball over the South African line. It wasn't allowed and the whistle went shortly afterward. I don't know whether it was frustration or tiredness or indignation at being robbed of a perfectly good try, but I rushed up to Max Baise and called him everything under the sun. I accused him of being a cheat and told him that even if Slattery had scored an unchallenged try he wouldn't, with the score at thirteen all, have awarded it. Oh dear! I felt so ashamed afterwards that I must have spent most of the evening apologizing to him. I still think that Fergus Slattery *did* score, but I shouldn't have spoken to the referee in that manner.

It was a genuine disappointment not to have taken a clean sheet home, but we had achieved a record that few expected of us when we flew to South Africa three months earlier. Though we were a party of whom none flinched from the challenges of South Africa, I for one cannot underestimate the contribution of Willie John McBride. This was the final tour for the big Irishman and he more than anyone developed a bond between individuals of varying talents, attitudes, backgrounds and emotions. Little wonder that the first person I sought for advice after being selected skipper of the 1977 Lions was Willie John.

My final match against the All Blacks—for Llanelli, October 1980

Mam and Dad with their 'Tamaid bach' (little one)

A friendly moment with Les, my father-in-law, who wasn't quite so friendly when I started courting his daughter

A happy reunion with Pat after the 1974 Lions tour

If they were only as quiet as that all of the time. The Bennett juniors, James and Steven

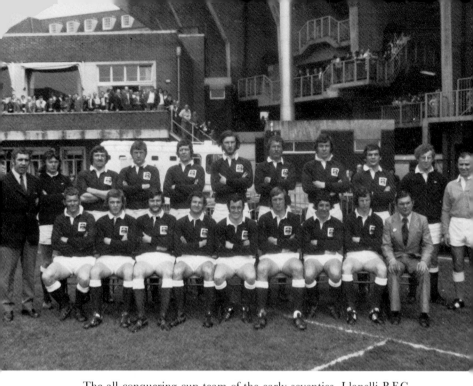

The all-conquering cup team of the early seventies. Llanelli RFC

'Llongyfarchiadau,' said Gareth on the phone, 'you're Captain.'

The ecstasy of victory for the Llanelli bench at the Llanelli–Aberavon Welsh Cup Final in 1974

The frustration of a drawn game against the Australians at Stradey Park

Probing the defences

Teaching Gareth the rudiments of accurate passing!

One of the memorable Llanelli moments. Scoring against the All White 'Jacks'!

Padded up for a celebration XI at Dafen C.C

Terry Griffiths came from Felinfoel you know!

The Prince of Wales shakes hands with one of his subjects—
Ray Gravell!

'Honestly, Ted, I am not at all interested in politics!'

'It's for Audrey, really!'

The Welsh 'tailor's dummy' team at No. 10, with James Callaghan towering over Gerald, J.J., Gareth and myself. From the left: J.P.R. Williams, Gerald Davies, Geoff Wheel, J.J. Williams, Gareth Edwards, Jeff Squire, Gerry Lewis, the Prime Minister James Callaghan, Charlie Faulkner, Phil Bennett, Steve Fenwick, Bobby Windsor and Ray Gravell

Above left: Bobby Windsor, a great man to have in your corner when the going gets rough

Above right: Willie John McBride. Simply, a great man

Below right: Derek Quinnell, a Lion for Llanelli, Wales and Britain

Below left: 'That bloody Dafydd Iwan maniac' — Ray Gravell. We sorely missed him in New Zealand

Above left: Safely on its way to touch. No doubt meeting the approval of Graham Price

Above right: 'Tell me "Duke", there's nothing in this Keane bloke is there?' Bobby 'Duke' Windsor and Geoff Wheel, the two comics of the Welsh team

Below: An opportunity for counterattacking against the All Blacks at Stradey Park in 1980

We tried convincing the All Blacks that Sid Going was the weak link. Brynmor Williams knew better!

Gareth Edwards with a try against England. The greatest 'poacher' of them all!

British Lions against the All Blacks in 1977. Too often we, the backs, let the forwards down

It's all up to us now. The 'donkeys' (Messrs Cobner, Quinnell, Faulkner and Squire) have done their bit

A dry surface against Auckland during the 1977 New Zealand tour. It was a rare occurrenc

7

Touring is Fun?

You need the bad times to appreciate the good 'uns, and you need bad tours to make you appreciate the enjoyable ones. As the memories fade, it's interesting to find that the humorous highlights are the ones that stay. Nevertheless, the Welsh tour of New Zealand in 1969 still haunts me and I'm not too enthusiastic about recalling journeys to Japan or Argentina either.

It is only now that administrators are beginning to realize what meticulous preparation is needed before embarking on international rugby tours. Acknowledging an itinerary as being acceptable without first-hand knowledge of the country's venues and the local circumstances, is nothing short of criminal. The Welsh administrators were guilty in all three of the countries that I've mentioned. The team was confined to a country house stuck in the middle of nowhere in Argentina; they were given the same hotel for the whole stay in Japan; and whoever planned the tour of New Zealand should have been lined up outside Cardiff Castle in a medieval stockade.

I wonder if it is asking too much of the overseers of such money-making tours to ponder a little before committing their gladiators to the arduous timetables. Though Wales went to New Zealand as conquerors of Europe and Home International champions in 1969, they were totally destroyed by a magnificent All Blacks team – helped by our own suicidal schedule. We had hardly recovered from a forty-two-hour flight when we were thrown into a hard provincial match against Taranaki. To make matters worse, four days after that we had to face New Zealand. The history books will tell you that we were taken to the cleaners; though no excuses should be offered, despite the best will in the world, the commitment needed was absent because of genuine tiredness.

The Welsh have acquired a reputation of being lousy travellers, an introspective lot given to homesickness and cliquish formation. I personally plead guilty to all charges of *hiraeth*, but on the two Lions tours that I've been on, I haven't seen any evidence to support the theory. I wonder, however, how many could withstand the boredom of same hotel and same routine that the Welsh players had to endure in Argentina. Goodness knows, I'm grateful for the opportunity of seeing the world and doing what I enjoy best, playing rugby, and it might seem less than charitable to criticize the people who spend a great deal of time organizing the tours. Nevertheless, there was little to do in the Argentinian country club except train, play golf and eat steaks. To those who would hold up their hands in horror at such ingratitude, there is a little saying in Welsh, '*Gormod o bwdin dagiff gi*,' which literally translated means 'Too much pudding will make even a dog sick'!

These short tours helped me to familiarize myself with the Welsh scene – the players, the administrators, and what was expected of the rugby tourist. I quickly appreciated too what a fine and inspiring captain John Dawes was in Argentina.

He must have been sorely tempted to call his men off in a number of the games there. Perhaps it is the Latin temperament, often quoted as the convenient excuse for shabby tactics used by the South Americans in most sports, but the dirty play and the lack of tight refereeing made the tour a nightmare. Though Ken John of the London referees joined us to see fair play in one match, he suddenly pulled a hamstring when Wales were 9 points to nil up. In no time at all, with some partisan decisions from the substituting Argentinian whistle-blower, the home side had pulled up to 14 all.

There is one incident that I shall treasure. The test match, as with all the other tour matches, was played in Buenos Aires. The stadium possessed a very short dead-ball area and a racing track. The Argentinians attempted a drop-goal which went wide of the posts and beyond the dead-ball line into the crowd. J.P.R. went to recover the ball from the crowd and threw it to me underneath the posts. With the Welsh forwards assembled for the twenty-five drop-out, I suddenly became aware of three Argentinians rushing towards me. Quickly realizing that they were not going to ask me the time of day, I scampered out of arm's reach. All my faculties weren't functioning properly and I tripped over and minored the ball. No one could believe the referee as he promptly whistled for a scrum 'five'. The Welsh pack went down bewildered ... And this was á test match!

The off-field activities were no more endearing. The ruthlessness of the country and its inhabitants could never have been better illustrated than during a visit to a cattle ranch. The scene was a colourful one, with cowboys on horseback, and a number of us had remarked on the elegance of one stallion. An attempt was made to capture him. Suddenly without warning the horse fell and broke a leg. The owner appeared to be deeply upset by the incident and much to our relief we were told that the animal would not be put down and all attempts would be made to 'fix' him. Fix him they did ... as we were about to leave, some of us witnessed that same man stick a knife in the horse's throat and the bloody wretchedness that followed would have sickened the hardiest of mortals. It is the volatile unpredictability which characterizes the Argentinian approach to the rugby game. The need for control and discipline is self-evident, but once achieved, it will make the Argentinians a potent force in the rugby arena.

No further evidence is needed of the Argentinian talent for the game than Hugo Porta. Of players from the so-called emerging rugby nations, he is by far the most talented three-quarter. To look at him you would think that he's been taught the ropes in one of our Welsh valleys, and there is no doubt that had he played in this country or in New Zealand he would have become an even greater player. Rugby in Argentina doesn't have the same pulling power as soccer and as such the rugby authorities there are merely looked upon as oddball game fanatics. At present, after the experiences of the Penguins, who rather foolishly tangled with the intolerant Argentinian authorities, I don't know whether it's a good place to tour. One thing is certain, they have little patience with anybody who tries to interfere with their national heritage, and that obviously includes street flags. It was because of this, perhaps, that the 1968 Welsh team were stuck in the country club.

There were some in that Welsh party who would have preferred a more physical game and, to the eternal credit of John Dawes, he resisted all attempts to turn the attitude of the Welsh party into a retaliatory expedition. Had the more senior men in the party employed a more physical attitude, heaven knows how the crowd, let alone the opposing players, would have reacted. In the first match the abiding memory is of one of their props being dragged off the field badly concussed. It was some time after the match, during the celebrations, that we heard that he had been taken to hospital and had tragically died. The instinctive reaction of the touring party was to leave the dinner there and then, lest the hosts with their fiery tongues take vengeance. However, we were told that the player had been kicked in the head by a horse a few months previously and that, in all probability, it was the severity of that blow that had caused his death. We were none too sure about accepting the explanation and weren't at all comfortable.

If it's lack of discipline that undermines the progress of Argentinian rugby, the Japanese have honourable credentials in that direction. Their talent in observing and copying commodities of the Western world is reflected even in their rugby. Scrummaging, mauling and rucking in the Japanese style might well have come out of those *Play Rugby This Way* manuals printed in the fifties. Their shortage of height and weight is a massive disadvantage which hardly looks as if it will be overcome in set-piece play. I wonder why they don't ask some of their Suma wrestlers to have a go, but as yet their teams have been subjected to some gruelling punishment merely because of their lack of size. That apart, they are clean and hospitable opponents, and I don't think their courage will ever be questioned. They paid Wales the honour of inviting us to the Land of the Rising Sun in 1975.

When it was announced that Les Spence would manage the tour of Japan, a few eyebrows were raised in the clubhouses of Welsh rugby. Les had been captured by the Japanese during the Second World War and, though he never mentioned that period of his life when travelling around, the memories of the treatment that he, and others, suffered during captivity must have been painful. But in my opinion his selection was a stroke of genius. The management of Lions tours needs a sustained degree of efficiency and diplomacy. On this and other short tours there is room for compassion to be shown to individuals who have given faultless service to the game. Les, a Cardiff man, was honoured in this way.

He took with him a collection of WRU pens. He quickly distributed these to every tour member but warned that failure to produce his pen on demand would cost the individual a round of drinks. Les, a lovable and scatterbrained sort of gentleman was of course the first to have to dip into his pocket at the bar. His team announcements had everyone in stitches. With glasses on the brink of his nose and paper in hand, he would authoritatively announce, 'That fellow from Swansea is one of the back row, you know who I mean don't you? Yes him, and he'll be partnered by . . . Who? I can't quite read this.'

John Dawes would try to quash the hysteric laughter with a team talk. Eventually the hilarity would subside and at the end of the talk, Les would rise to thank John, 'I would like to thank Jack Daw for his contribution.' And the team would collapse once again. He also went to great pains to help the players, and at times his solicitousness cost him dearly. At the end of the tour Charlie Faulkner approached Customs at Heathrow with about forty-three bags underneath his arms, a present for every club member in Pontypool!

The customs officer lurched forward amazed at the spectacle and looked as if he was about to bolster Her Majesty's coffers with a not inconsiderable contribution from Charlie. However 'Spence', spotting the danger, leapt in front of Charlie with his own bags, giving the rest of us a welcome chance to slip past. Les, crestfallen, rejoined us in the bus later. 'That dreadful fellow charged me for just about everything I had.' Poor old Les, but what a marvellous comradeship we shared with him.

However, when he and John 'Sid' Dawes walked into my hotel room in Hong Kong one morning I thought that my career in Welsh rugby was over, and I was to be banished from the scene. I had been told that I was to captain Wales in the first tour match against the local Hong Kong fifteen. The news was something to celebrate since it was my first captaincy and, though John Dawes asked me not to go overboard with the celebrations, there were three days to go and the advice, I'm afraid, was ignored.

At four a.m. Geoff Wheel, inspired by a skiffle group and aided by Australian beer, was on a table doing a 'Swansea dockland' tap-dance. The entertainment was greatly appreciated by the lads if no one else. At the precise moment that John Dawes walked into the room, 'Wheelo' crashed through the timber. Sid looked over at me and simply said 'And you're the captain?'

I knew I'd had it, and the tour would probably turn sour for me. The next day during the training session John didn't speak to me; it was noticeable, too, that Mervyn Davies the tour captain was distant. I confided in Gareth, who told me not to worry, but I had a nagging feeling that severe disciplinary measures were about to be announced. On the morning of the match, there was a knock on the door and in walked the management. I thought, This is it, I'm to be sent home. I had a mental picture of Pat waiting at Heathrow with a twelve-bore shotgun at the ready.

Les had a piece of paper in his hand.

'Do you mind awfully if you could stand down as captain? Geoff Wheel has sunburn, Derrick Quinnell has moved to number four and Mervyn as tour captain will have to come in at number eight. Do you mind, Phil?'

Mind? I didn't mind at all ... the relief on my face must have been obvious because Sid, unable to restrain himself any longer, burst out laughing.

He was less amused when a number of us took to two-wheeler transport on the Tokyo highways. We'd been to a Berni Inn. It had been a comfortable evening, with Charlie Faulkner trying to remember the second verse of 'There's a hole in my bucket', and Geoff Wheel giving everybody his one-man show. There was a bit of devilry in the air.

The walk from the restaurant to the hotel was quite some distance and, in no time at all, Allan Martin had found a small pushbike somewhere and was speeding along the road. The others needed no further prompting. Bikes were acquired and 'Panther' Martin led the way. However, as we turned around the corner into the hotel forecourt, I caught a glimpse of Allan and Sid Dawes having a rare old linguistic confrontation with the local police. Allan had obviously been caught. I wasn't quick enough to avoid the attention of one of the officers but, dispensing with my bike, I managed to get into the lift and hid underneath the bed for what seemed to be an eternity.

Pandemonium had broken loose downstairs. As soon as Sid had managed to convince the police that there would be no repetition of such juvenile behaviour, Graham 'Surtees' Price rode around the corner. Reliable witnesses tell me that he muttered something like 'Hands off' to the excitable policeman; but they were incensed by this time and wanted to take all three of us in for questioning. I still don't know how it was resolved or how we were able to escape the penalties of the Japanese judicial system. I suspect that Allan Martin broke down and confessed and asked for other offences to be considered against him!

On the field of play it was farcical. The scores against the Japanese were gigantic and there was little we could do but apologize afterwards. It was no fun scoring sixty or eighty points against opposition who had neither the ability nor the strength to compete. Neither could you ask the Welsh team to deflate their competitive spirit; that would have been even more insulting. The Japanese took it very badly and after one of the test matches, which we'd won by eighty-six points, their players were sent to bed at an incredibly early hour.

If Les Spence dominated the stage at the team meetings, Geoffrey Wheel was in every sense the joker of the pack. What a marvellous individual he is and, though he loses himself in the heat of the battle at times, a more considerate human being would be difficult to find. He is something of a worrier, and I've no doubt that he would worry about the opposition even if he was playing against the Old Anselmians fifths in a public park. I can remember him now pacing up and down the dressing room in Japan.

'Let me at 'em, nothing in these Japanese. I'll get amongst them. Nothing to them at all. Come on boys, you follow me!'

The entire team broke down with laughter when, after that particular 'Wheelo' tirade, he was floored five minutes into the game by an immaculate punch delivered by a five-feet-six Japanese frame. As is so often the case, Wheelo, who has an eccentric nature, is given to moments of self-doubt too. The supply of letters on that Japanese trip was sporadic and it was yet another annoying feature of the organization of the tour. I, for one, love to have letters sent from home because they not only provide me with news of my children, they are totally necessary for my morale. However Geoffrey hadn't received a single communication from his wife for ten days and the strain was beginning to tell.

'I tell you, she's gone off with the milkman! I'll murder her and him when I get home.'

Such was his mood of bitterness that Les Spence had to plead with him not to misbehave at a British embassy reception that we were asked to attend. Despite the lack of communication with his dear one at home, he was still in a fairly genial mood and went through the usual Wheel diplomatic routine of asking where they kept their sandwiches as soon as we'd entered the foyer. The embassy staff were very apologetic about the delay in the post, but a large delivery had arrived that morning, not an unsubstantial number of which were for the Swansea lock. Of course, this brought a great howl of delight from Geoff as he left for a small private corner to digest all the home news. 'There you are, I told you she loved me, didn't I?'

He's much the same as Ray Gravell – a worrier. I remember on a Barbarians tour of Canada, where tradition in the party dictated that, since we had no coach, the selection of the Baa-Baas' team was a players' committee responsibility. The rugby wasn't all that taxing, and with a heavy concentration of talent in the party we were well equipped to take care of ourselves. Some of us did tend to indulge a little too much in the generous Canadian hospitality . . . and indeed Geoff Wheel was developing a sizeable gut. Mike Biggar was the first to pass comment on the new Wheel physique. The Wheel response was 'Tell Kojak that we are here for fun.' But more in jocularity than concern, I did, as captain, have a quiet word with Geoff about the additional weight. What a response!

Grav, J.J. and myself were enjoying a quiet swim in the team hotel pool. Suddenly, the air was filled with a noise that none of us had ever heard before. It resembled something between human wailing and a bull calf in trouble. It was quite frightening, and it suggested that someone was in trouble. Quickly we tried to discover the source of the noise so that we could render any assistance to the sufferer. Eventually we came to the conclusion that the noise, now having attracted a considerable amount of interest among the other hotel guests, was coming from the hotel's gym and sauna room. Further investigation revealed Mr Wheel inside the sauna room, close to terminal exhaustion having spent a considerable amount of time in the punishing heat, pedalling away on an exercise bike. The gut *and* Geoff Wheel had almost vanished for ever.

Quite probably the most humiliating Welsh tour that took place was the 1969 tour of New Zealand. The All Blacks in that year exposed the Welsh limitations in an efficient and agonizing manner. Wales arrived in New Zealand heralded as European champions, and indeed there were some who described that Welsh team as one of the finest. Maurice Richards and Gerald Davies had become world-class three-quarters, the partnership of Barry and Gareth was beginning to flourish and the Welsh pack had driven all before it in the home championship. The All Blacks had digested on such claims for months before our arrival and any pretenders to the throne of world rugby had to be dealt with in a severe manner. The All Blacks achieved their goal. Wales were humiliated in two defeats: 19 to 0 and 33 to 12.

The arrangements for that visit were quiet chaotic, with Wales playing an important provincial match against Taranaki after a gruelling flight from the other side of the world. The preparation was limited and the actual schedule showed a complete lack of foresight. Nevertheless I can't put the entire blame on the travelling arrangements, nor shall I attempt to do so. The New Zealanders were magnificent and we needed a tactical plan in order to stop or divert the play from their strength . . . their fearsome pack. There was a necessity for some analytical thinking, and I'm afraid that this was lacking. An additional problem was the questionable commitment of some of the Welsh touring party. A number of them had seen many a memorable battle and were approaching the end of distinguished careers, and there just wasn't enough resilience in the party to compete against the endless energy of the All Blacks. The retirement announcements of a few of the players were hastened by that tour.

Even coach Clive Rowlands, the world's best motivator – even he could not summon the 'dog' that was needed. There was a need in the three-quarters for someone of the calibre of John Dawes to assert his presence; he was clearly the best general of the backs, even in 1969. John was, however, thankful for his place on tour and content to take any games that were offered him. It all went so drastically wrong; only a handful of the party did anything to enhance their reputations as Wales slid to two colossal defeats. J.P.R. won the respect of the crowds with his madcap heroics, Gerald was seen too rarely to become appreciated, and only Mervyn Davies and Norman Gale produced the effort needed to confront these raging All Blacks. Colin Meads the New Zealand skipper accused the Welsh of not competing or combating, which was a sour pill to swallow, and the inevitable oral attack and counterattack ensued between the two camps. It would have been better perhaps to take the hiding and head for home.

However, too much was said by a number of people and those who wonder why relations between Wales and New Zealand deteriorated so much in the 1970s can refer back to the press coverage given to the Welsh team in 1969. Much of what was said was justified, since we were a very poor team indeed but, as soon as the knife began to turn, irresponsible comments from the Welsh camp merrily kept the typewriters fuming.

What a relief it was to snatch a victory over the Australians and then move on to the palm trees of Fiji. Ivor Jones, the WRU president from Gorseinon, wouldn't agree since he was the first to taste the mud-coloured drink of welcome from the islanders.

'*Beth uffern yw hwn,*' were the words of Welsh exclamation that voiced his suspicion that the Fijians were about to avenge the exploits of Captain Cook. But after the exposure and inquisition of New Zealand, Fiji, as always, was a delightful experience. The memories of Keith Jarrett refusing to train because of the continual presence of toads on the ground, the sight of Norman Gale in Fijian national dress and the meanderings of Chico Hopkins in the market towns looking for bargain spears; they all come flooding back. It's a marvellous place for gift-hunters, as all Lions tourists to the Antipodes have found, but poor old Maurice Richards, having bought an expensive engagement present, was a dead giveaway to the Customs officers as he stuttered through his explanation. Maurice insisted that if we'd won both our tests in New Zealand he'd have been allowed through trouble free.

The intake of the warm Fijian air did a great deal to heal the wounds inflicted by the All Blacks of 1969. A return visit to the islands in 1977 was just as enjoyable and made us all think that we should re-examine our attitude towards the game, and the matches between rival countries. The 'win at all costs' attitude has reduced many a game to a barbaric exhibition of strength and to 'who can get away with what' exploits. If we are to succeed in attracting the schoolchildren into the game what shall we show them – video tapes of the Lions of 1977? England in Australia? Ireland against Wales in 1978? Or the worst example of all – Wales against England in 1980? We should co-opt the Fijians and the Japanese into our deliberations to remind ourselves what made the game so attractive in the first place.

The experiences of the Welsh clubs in South Africa during the summer of 1979 offer no solution to the problems of rugby aggression. Cardiff and Newport certainly had to fight through their campaigns and Llanelli were involved in more rugged encounters than I'd witnessed, after more than twelve years of playing for them. Because of the lack of international competition, matches against the rare touring-club teams take on different dimensions in South Africa. The South Africans' training is quite incredible. By the time they've finished their three-hour stints, all the rugby has been run out of them. They are not helped either by some indifferent refereeing.

Our tour match against South Western Districts was extraordinary. We'd been denied the services of our international quartet of Quinnell, Allan Martin, Paul Ringer and J.J. The younger players in the club were left with the responsibility of facing what we were told was a fairly respectable provincial team. The play was nothing short of vicious. The referee was totally out of his depth as he tried to create some semblance of order out of infernal chaos. After a particularly bloody encounter, John 'Coch' Williams our prop was sent into the experimental 'sin bin'. It seemed quite amusing at the time to see this burly fellow trudge into the lawmakers' novel implement but it was some twenty minutes later, when Gareth Jenkins broke his hand on somebody's jaw, that the referee suddenly remembered the plight of John Williams – he even had to be reminded of the 'sin bin'.

The 'sin bin' is no answer. Other referees, I've no doubt, would have been far more efficient but, when a man has squandered much of the game in the solitude of a no-go area, the corrective measure doesn't have the desired effect. I remember John hitting the first scrum after his reprieve like a raging bull. The standard of sportsmanship in all the major rugby-playing countries has deteriorated rapidly, and the situation is getting out of hand. If the 'sin bin' was effective as a corrective measure, I would be in favour of its introduction. But the punishment may well serve as a catalyst for further aggression.

Happily, not all tours are dominated by misdemeanours and flashes of temperament and intolerance on the playing fields. The socializing and the post-match parties and dinners are always moments to treasure.

Sadly, though, even these in the past few years have become overburdened by weak people who have harboured trivial dislikes and prejudices after the game until joviality becomes contrived rather than natural.

Funnily enough, one of my most amusing tour anecdotes comes not from the confines of a New Zealand or a South African hotel but from the rugby stronghold of Guernsey!

It wasn't a difficult tour for the Llanelli club and nearly all of us had gone there with the sole intention of enjoying ourselves. Most of us accomplished the task well. However there was one reception to get through before we could really let our hair down. Guernsey RFC had extended an invitation to the touring party to join them for a fairly informal reception. Glan Tucker the tour manager would have none of the the 'informal' bit, and ordered us all to dress in club blazers, and to be there at the clubhouse spick and span and sober. A few of the younger element had gone off with Gareth Jenkins promising that they wouldn't do anything daft before arriving at the clubhouse.

When the time came to set off for the reception there were merely a handful present, much to the chagrin of Glan and our host in Guernsey, Graham Jenkins (Richard Burton's brother). The clubhouse was situated in a delightful spot (it was part of a sporting complex) and in true colonial fashion we sipped our drinks watching a cricket game in the distance. Eventually the blazer-wearers and the officials retired inside to offer our official thank-yous to the Guernsey people. I was in the middle of my short speech when I spotted across the cricket boundary a Mini being driven precariously close to the white-flannelled players. From where I stood I could just about make out that there must have been some six or seven men inside the car. On top there were five people that I could identify as our 'missing' tour party. As yet the official reception hadn't been alerted, and I tried to carry on stretching out my speech in the vain hope that no one would notice the antics of the irreverent bunch behind them. The Mini turned around and the bowler was suddenly confronted by a deserted wicket, his fielders leaping for safety and British Leyland's finest product with eleven people on board ready at the crease. They arrived at the reception very much the worse for wear and Glan Tucker didn't know where to put himself. Apologies were made ... but I must admit that the sight of that lot careering towards the wicket had an element of the 'Carry On' films about it.

Tours need their high jinks and their characters in order to sustain and highlight the good nature of the participants. The responsibility of representing one's country or club should be sufficient to keep irresponsible acts in check, though this theory can be, and has been, severely tested by the unwarranted acts of vandalism carried out by the few on every tour. On the lengthy tour, boredom and frustration are the premier causes of hose-pipe incidents and the midnight prowling. It is all very well for the 'concerned' journalist to wax lyrical about the immaturity of certain players and the nonsensical acts performed by grown-up men, but to be confined in the psychological claustrophobia of a three month tour is enough to tax the most levelheaded of any group of individuals. I've often noticed that the journalists suffer in the same way. As the tour progresses into the latter half, it becomes abundantly clear that the scribes are grateful for any crumb of copy; if there's nothing forthcoming, the worst trivia is placed under intense magnification and the truth distorted out of all proportion. The touring alliance between player and journalist, as was witnessed during 1977, is an uneasy one. The 1977 experience was not, however, entirely the fault of the press boys.

8

All Blacks '77

I should never have accepted the captaincy of the British Lions tour of New Zealand in 1977. I have no desire to appear ungracious, ungrateful, or play the role of the unlikely hero, but I've spent many a wistful hour thinking of what could have been achieved had the leadership gone to someone far better equipped than I to deal with the all-engulfing pressures of a three-month rugby expedition. By the end of our stay in New Zealand I had no desire to stay in that country since I now knew that all my weaknesses as a player and tourist were exposed in that short time. While I admit that I was a bad choice for the captaincy, there were others too on that tour who have cause to regret the events of 1977.

To bear malice against individuals rarely achieves anything, but so many have privately and publicly pointed accusing fingers toward a number of people involved on that tour that it is high time that the record was set straight. I have had to accept criticisms that I was neither physically nor mentally strong enough to suffer the punishment of that New Zealand tour, which rarely presented us with a dry pitch and towards the end brought its daily internal strife. I would, on reflection, endorse those criticisms. To captain Wales in the home international championship is a responsibility that carries its own pressures. The build-up starts on the Thursday but by the Saturday both mind and body should be attuned to the task of playing international rugby. It is an exacting experience and a challenge that is always difficult to cope with, but it eventually becomes easier with experience. There are those who appear to be unaffected by it all – the Barry Johns and the Steve Fenwicks of this world – though even they burn a little before each match. On the other hand each single match on a British Lions tour is an international, and no one is capable of maintaining the desired peak of performance in every game. My own form in New Zealand deteriorated badly towards the latter end of the tour, a result of injury, homesickness and, above all I think, the shackles of captaincy.

When I was first phoned up at home by John Dawes and told of the appointment, I admit I reached a state of euphoria. Others had been mentioned for the skipper role – Uttley of England, Ian McGeechan of Scotland – and I knew that but for the cruel injury to Mervyn Davies, he would have been an automatic choice. But after putting the phone down I knew that I'd arrived at the top of the tree – Felinfoel CP, Coleshill, Llanelli and District Schools, Welsh Youth, Wales and now – the envied position of all rugby players. I gave little thought in the next few days as to whether I was suitable enough for the job.

As I've mentioned before, I had derived enormous pleasure in South Africa but my sole ambition under Willie John had been to play for a place in the test team. In New Zealand, the poacher-turned-gamekeeper had a thousand and one things to think about besides concentrating on winning the series.

Ironically, my first task was to persuade Llanelli centre Ray Gravell that he should make himself available. He'd been injured during the season but the Lions management had told me that they were keen to have him in the party providing he could prove his fitness. It so happened that we had a game against Maesteg shortly before the Lions selection and I tried moving heaven and earth to get Ray to play. He would have none of it, and decided not to play. So John Dawes wasted a journey. There were many moments when a number of us on tour, bruised from the onslaught of Bill Osborne and Bruce Robertson, reflected on how Ray would have enjoyed 'eating them up'.

Gareth, J.P.R., Gerald, Peter Dixon and Fergus Slattery had all made themselves unavailable – five players who on paper would have been prominent contenders for the test matches. Their decisions to stay at home I respected, though their presence would have been invaluable and crucial. If the tour had been shorter, one or two of them might possibly have been persuaded to go, but I suspect that even such a magnificent competitor as Gareth had sincere reservations about being hounded by New Zealand back-rows for three months. 'Think of me having a pint in Porthcawl, Phil *bach*, when you're running up those sand-dunes in Otago.' I often thought of Gareth and his Porthcawl pint ... in fact there were times when I thought of little else.

Though I think that Gareth might not have lasted the tour as well as he did in South Africa, we needed him badly in New Zealand. There were times when the tactical kick was needed, the threat of a run and, more essentially, the presence of mind to dictate when the tide was going against us. He was also a marvellous tourist and had a wealth of experience with which to steady the nerves of the newcomers, of whom there were several.

The other four too would have given us that badly missed nucleus of experienced tourists.

As it was I had reservations about some selections which bordered on nationalistic naïvety. It was not a selection that truly reflected the strength of the home championship teams.

I'd had little to do with 'Dodd' Burrell before the team was announced. We had met on a few occasions and discussed the availability of players but I wasn't a party to the eventual team selection. Perhaps, given the withdrawal of the players that I've mentioned, it was virtually a process of picking those who were willing to travel. Despite the fact that scrummaging became our forte in New Zealand I think the Scottish front-row (notably Ian

McLauchlan) felt justifiably aggrieved at being ignored. The first few weeks in New Zealand under the management of George Burrell were pleasant and agreeable. Towards the end, however, probably because of the claustrophobia that affected us all and the pressure of being in the limelight, George allowed what I feel were petulant matters to dominate the running of the team, which jeopardized the welfare of his fellow tourists. Our appreciation of the hospitality offered was, in my view, not fully conveyed because of his reluctance to play a public relations role.

A fair proportion of the time on tour is inevitably spent with the travelling press corps. Now more than ever before, the rugby media has an insatiable thirst for mere titbits of information and that is why the player has the responsibility of watching every word he offers in discussions. There are members of the press that I can honestly trust not to divulge private conversations in print. Many have been friends for a long time and I know that if the inadvertent clanger were dropped, a few eyebrows would be raised, but discreet diplomacy observed and the confidence of the friendship never jeopardized. Sometimes, you can get caught out. I well remember having what I assumed to be a convivial and private chat with John Reason of the *Daily Telegraph*, who questioned me about my thoughts of the South African three-quarters in 1974. I spoke quite honestly and suggested that they lacked flair and ability in loose situations. Much to my eternal regret, I never thought for a minute that John would report our tête-à-tête, but he did ... and time has still not healed that wound. He'll never be on any dinner list of mine. Unless an individual pressman transgresses that thin diplomatic line, he is always welcome in my company. On the New Zealand tour, as far as John Dawes was concerned, most of the press had transgressed that line just by their mere presence.

It was a continual running war between 'Sid' Dawes and the media boys, with a number of the battles being fought in the early hours when tongues, and shirt collars were loose. It was well known that we, as players, were not encouraged to speak to the press. The policy was quite unreasonable since a number of the media gang were friends of a number of players and have remained so since the tour. Yet for pressmen to be seen by the management fraternizing with the likes of Barry John, Clem Thomas, Carwyn James and Mervyn Davies was tantamount to high treason. It was all very childish.

Why the friction should have occurred at all is a mystery to me. John had been here before in his successful role as the 1971 Lions captain and knew better than any of us what to expect from the All Black players and the New Zealand critics and public. At home he had captained and coached the Welsh team for the best part of a decade, so being under the spotlight was no new experience for him. Yet in New Zealand he became sensitive to the slightest criticism. He developed a paranoia about the press party, and had all the Lions rugby articles published in Britain sent to him wherever we were. It seemed to some of the senior players that he was intent on staging a private war against the journalists. In these battles John certainly played the role of 'general' and George the manager became very much the bewildered 'colonel'. Some of the confrontations were ugly, and gradually the concern about the stability of the management crept into the Lions party. Early on in the tour several players came to me to express their disgust at the bar-room slanging matches and the discourtesy shown to people who knew as much as any of us about the game and who had a right to express their opinions. It was a sad reflection that before the end of the tour a number of the Lions had more or less sent their coach to Coventry ... it was all so pointless.

Let me hasten to add that I could have been of little support to John in all this turmoil. My own form deteriorated badly in the second half of the tour (the injury to my shoulder after being accidentally felled by Willie Duggan didn't help) but perhaps if the party as a whole had been a happier one the will and the commitment to win could have been healthier.

The conditions were awful. We had a hint of the weather to come in our very first game against Waiarabush at Masterton. A freezing wind together with large pools of water and face-burning sleet and rain greeted the 1977 Lions on their first trial of the tour. Conditions hardly got better and the tour suffered because of it. Acclimatizing to such conditions after a winter of rugby in Wales wasn't at all difficult, but the monotony of dragging one's body through quagmire after quagmire and having to train in togs that were always sodden, eventually tarnished the glitter of being on a Lions tour. Already we had suffered crucial blows before boarding the plane to New Zealand. Roger Uttley was forced to withdraw because of back trouble at our medical session at Twickenham and Geoff Wheel, after a mysterious sequence of examinations, was advised to pull out after heart trouble was diagnosed. Both were replaced by fine players – Jeff Squire and Moss Keane – but the touring party had already been unsettled. I, more than anybody, knew what a major blow it was not to have Roger Uttley on tour. I had already singled him out as my pack 'shop steward'.

The next injury victim was poor old Elgan Rees, who seemed to attract misfortune in the mould of the Denis the Menace of old. Then, hardly a match went by without some minor or major injury affecting our selection alternatives. And the casualty list included some key members of the touring party.

We were none too impressive in the first quartet of matches against New Zealand opposition. Sometimes we received the occasional nod of approval from former All Blacks and critics, but there was a general lack of conviction about our play. Whereas Carwyn in 1971 had a fairly good idea of who to pick for his teams in the early matches, injuries – and possibly a lack of analytical planning – prevented us from settling into a cohesive unit. There were the odd moments of inspiration when the jelling of forward competitiveness and thrustful three-quarter play came together, but even after romping home by 60 points against the Wanganui-King Country team (coached by Colin Meads), I had an uneasy feeling that we were conning ourselves ... there was an ingredient missing. My fears were confirmed when one or two of the pack suggested that someone or something had to be done about our forward play. So far, we had shown only a reasonable account of our potential up front. Since the back play was at best only adequate, with the exception of Andy Irvine, something had to be done. Even John Dawes conceded that the master plan had been jolted by the impressive displays of Taranaki and Hawke's Bay. The scoreboard at the end of those two games showed slender winning margins and the date of the first test match was fast approaching.

I have yet to be convinced that three-quarters who become coaches have the slightest idea of what forward play is all about. No matter how many manuals, lectures or seminars are absorbed, unless the coach has first-hand knowledge of the frustrations and nuances of front-row or lock play, how on earth can he expect to gain the respect of his forward unit. I have seen and heard coaches graduate from the WRU system and even I, with my limited knowledge of forward play, can recognize their limitations. Carwyn in 1971 enlisted the help of Ray MacLaughlan to help him with the pack. Conversely Syd Millar, who needed no schoolboy manual on the art of scrummaging, in 1974 turned to Gareth and J.P.R. in order to get the three-quarters sorted out. Eventually John, or rather the players, looked to Terry Cobner to whip the 1977 pack into shape. It was a promotion that should have come earlier, and yet ironically it was the three-quarters who lacked the techniques in New Zealand and not the pack. The men up front were magnificent.

By the time we met Otago, a provincial team renowned for its rucking, the forwards had come to terms with the New Zealand opposition. Sadly something else had also emerged. In the game against Manawatu, the Ranfurly shieldholders, their scrum-half Mark Donaldson kicked Willie Duggan in the head. From where I was it seemed a deliberate kick to the head, but despite the fact that the referee was only a few yards away the crime went unpunished and, what is more, went largely unreported in the New Zealand press. The crime was symbolic of the growing resentment against the Lions. Newspaper reports had already started carrying stories of our boorish attitude towards the game; one paper in particular had published accounts of late-night parties which were simply untrue. It hardened our attitude, but the die of animosity had been cast and it was going to get a lot worse.

We were, however, gradually getting our game right, and despite the narrow victories against Otago and Southland there was confidence in the party. Rivalry for places in the test side was intense, the hooking position was a private matter between Peter Wheeler and Bobby Windsor. The two locks, now that most of the available men were fit, were anybody's guess, so too were the back row and the two wings. But whatever confidence had been generated by the improvement in our forward play was destroyed against the New Zealand Universities.

There was an inevitable temptation to relax against the Universities. After all, they were a team that had hardly played together . . . an unknown force. By the end of the match the Lions had been outwitted and outfought. We weren't even in the game, as the students worried and harrassed us into making elementary mistakes. We lost the game and it was a shattering blow to our pride and to our preparation for the test match.

After the Universities game John Dawes murdered us. There are times when I find it difficult to remember matches or individual incidents, but when I'm old and grey I shall remember the morning after the match against the students with total clarity. It was the most painful session that I've ever encountered.

I don't know whether John meant it as punishment or

119

whether he thought our fitness on tour was questionable but to see nearly the full complement of the touring party begging for mercy sprawled across the field must have left the New Zealand spectators bewildered.

The training field was quite near the hotel, but a river prevented easy access. The exercises went on and on, until those feeling squeamish had no alternative but to be ill right there and then. Some were even crying, but there was no sign of a respite as the orders rolled off the tongue. I remember a stage when, even as a captain, I was moved to protest.

'Get on with it,' came the reply. Somehow I found a small reserve of strength....

After what seemed to be an eternity, he sent us on a half-mile run. Only the hard of hearing could have avoided picking up the insults being hurled at him. But John wasn't finished yet.

'Right, don't lie there, fifty press-ups!'

It was unbelievable ... and the sight of Allan Martin cussing and swearing would have put anybody off the game of rugby football. At this stage of the proceedings I didn't know whether there was any point to it all ... certainly John would have a hard time now convincing any of us that there was a motive behind the punishment. But it had its humour when eventually he relented and sent us back into the hotel. Remember the river? Some of the boys were so shattered that the thought of walking to the bridge presented too much of a challenge. So walk waist-deep through the still waters we did.

The team for the first test was picked and after the torture session we did no more than relax before the game. The first international will be remembered for the Grant Batty interception. The ball came out to the Lions three-quarters and Grant Batty, despite being confronted with an overlap, read the situation and caught the pass meant for me. It was a stunning blow, especially since we were within a whisper of winning. I would be the first to admit that they had the better of us up front, but until that little resourceful fellow latched onto the ball, the game so easily could have been ours. However, I was more than a little concerned about personal matters. In trying to stop an inevitable try by the All Blacks scrum-half, Willie Duggan had fallen on my shoulder and the pain was acute. I stayed on the field to play the full eighty minutes but soon afterwards doctors were talking of putting me in plaster and indeed my future participation in the tour seemed doubtful. But it was eventually decided to let matters be and see if therapeutic treatment to the shoulder could bring recovery.

The mood of the other boys after the first test defeat was strange. Though we had been beaten we gradually convinced ourselves during the evening's post-mortems that we could do better, that we had the beating of the All Blacks. In all credit to 'Dod' Burrell and John, they rallied around the party and there were no recriminations.

'From here we have to pick ourselves up,' said John, and there was general agreement that it was quite possible.

That first defeat affected the press party in a different way. It had given them licence to print everything that they had thought had gone wrong with the tour so far. Whatever John Dawes did during that part of the tour, his loyalty to the players was never in doubt. The same compliment couldn't be paid to some of the journalists. One New Zealand publication, *Truth*, blasted us with all kinds of allegations. We were told of orgies and drinking parties that we were supposed to have been going on since we first set foot in New Zealand. Most of the articles were written by a chap called Metlock. I was often left wondering how he could sleep at night knowing how much imaginative rubbish he'd written for the so-called rugby-following public. He never asked questions at press conferences, never came to see the management to check facts, but, though we discussed taking legal action against him and his paper, it would have only served to bolster his circulation figures.

121

Dealing with the New Zealand press was one matter. To be betrayed by one of your own was far more damaging. Tony Bodley of the *Daily Express* had also filed critical copy which had our management fuming. It was decided by one and all to send Tony Bodley to Coventry for a while, and he was told in no uncertain terms how we viewed his betrayal. Criticisms about tactical play on the field we could take and, if the Lions weren't playing well, we knew what to expect from the press. But a few criticisms bordered on that shady area of sports news coverage, and, if journalists were granted the privilege of our confidence we expected that confidence to be honoured. But the two incidents were the first of many, and the rift between the Lions party and the accompanying journalists grew even wider. These incidents also had a detrimental effect on the New Zealand public and the 'in' thing was now to 'hate' the Lions.

We have seen similar aggressive attitudes towards the All Blacks in this country and I make no apology for the disgust that I feel when I see a red-scarved Welshman or a black-capped New Zealander showing the worst of human traits. Over the past decade the Welsh have been served with success, and at times they have not only become bad losers but also intolerable winners. The New Zealand supporters during the 1977 tour were of much the same mould. By the time that the second test had arrived, we had reached the stage when the Lions were being spat upon, cans were thrown at us, and the language used against us wasn't even fit for a Christchurch gutter. I obviously exclude the genuinely hospitable hosts from these observations, but many a time when the rain drove us all to the confines of the bedroom I was left to reflect on the quality of sportsmanship on that tour. Where on earth was the good humour of the 1955 Lions that I'd read about? Why had we become so hated? Was it really all about nationalistic pride and not the amateur game? Perhaps it was my naïvety that prompted me to ask such questions. I remember Barry John after his retirement tell me of the contempt he'd felt when watching a crowd

of Welsh supporters disgrace themselves at Twickenham. 'You know,' he said, 'if I thought that I was out
there playing for that mob, I would have packed up a
long time ago.'

Fortunately with the ever-telling influence of Terry
Cobner as the 'general' of the forwards, the Lions began
to realize a certain amount of their potential ... though
the bad weather doggedly refused to desert us.

The other problem that by now we seemed unable to
escape was the smear stories. 'LIONS ARE WRECKERS',
'LIONS ARE CHARGED WITH ASSAULT', 'LIONS ARE
ANIMALS': these were the headlines that fed the public of
New Zealand as we prepared for a match that we had to
win to keep the series alive. One incident illustrates
perfectly the smears. On the Sunday in our Wellington
hotel, the hotel manager had, for some reason, closed the
bar and there were quite a few of us feeling a little
dehydrated and in sad need of refreshment. So Fran
Cotton and one or two other gentlemen 'lifted' the bar
gate and we helped ourselves to what was available. At
first, the manager was angry with us, but after we'd
convinced him that we would all contribute towards the
Cotton damage, he quickly seized upon the chance to
make himself a fortune by keeping the party well supplied with stocks. In fact it was one of the more pleasant
of the impromptu gatherings, with the manager's till
singing away to his unexpected afternoon rush. Two
days later someone made another killing, but this time of
another sort. There in the morning press blared the
headline, 'LIONS WRECK HOTEL BAR'. Absolutely amazing ... I only hope that whoever it was made enough
money out of the story.

The second test match at Christchurch was brutal.
Late tackles and charges, with a degree of incompetent
refereeing from Mr Duffy, allowed the game to deterior-
ate into an exchange of fury between the two teams who
had little respect for the basics of rugby. The conditions
again were atrocious, but the exchanges up front were
even more unpalatable.

123

Whatever had initially caused such a collision of bad temper was really inconsequential since both teams, as the game progressed, were equally guilty of dishing it out.

Graham Price's face was torn apart. As for myself, after being tackled on the ground and feeling a kick nicking my face, I just wondered what on earth I was doing 13,000 miles from home subjecting myself to this sort of thing. However, we were in the lead and the New Zealanders were making a hash of things. Bryan Williams was having an off day with his kicking, and Sid Going was misusing the ball. The Lions pack, though well beaten in the line-outs, were putting on a magnificent performance and the three-quarters were tackling everything in sight. The onslaught on the Lions line towards the end of the game, with the New Zealanders 13 to 9 down, was exhausting, but somehow we kept them at bay. That particular performance summed up the courage of the Lions who, when assembled in the changing room afterwards, would have done a casualty ward proud. Mud, blood, bandages and smiles greeted the visitor as we silently knew that the show was back on the road again.

Next door the casualties numbered just about the same, but the feelings were of wounded pride and deep disappointment.

We were level in the series and, even if the cynics attributed our win to New Zealand errors, we didn't care, it was there on the scoreboard, which for this touring side was very important indeed.

The celebrations were for once uninhibited. Then, after the test match, it was a welcome change to play a match in good spirit. That is precisely what happened in the following match against the Maoris where Sid Going, smarting from criticism after Saturday's game, used all his guile and wit in trying to motivate his Maori team. It was a good win for the Lions this one since it set us up for the games against Waikato, the Juniors and Auckland.

The weather and injuries, however, in the period between the second and third test, were to prove crucial not only to the size of our playing complement but to the morale of the squad as well. First Clive Williams received an injury which was to keep him out of the game for the rest of the tour; then Brynmor Williams, who had been worthy of a medal for all that he suffered on tour, went off with a hamstring pull; David Burcher also retired from the Waikato game as did Jeff Squire. The following match against the Juniors is best remembered from photographs taken on the touchline – not one of the forwards on either side was recognizable after ten minutes. How the Lions forwards pushed the Juniors! But as we slithered from scrum to maul, we questioned if the game should have been played at all. It was in games such as these when one wondered whether the rugby authorities had any right at all to demand such arduous tours from the players. I think, with all due respect to the New Zealand Rugby Union, that if the 1977 tour could have been shortened by at least eight games it would have become a far more spectacular event, though perhaps not as profitable. Employers, wives and children have to put up with a great deal with players who ask to be relieved of responsibilities so that they can kick a ball around in foreign parts for three months. I wonder if the Lions attitude towards the tour would have been healthier had the tour been shortened or, more significantly, would those who declared themselves unavailable have been more prepared to travel to New Zealand had it been an eighteen-match event?

Just before the third test we suffered a major blow. That amazing competitor Cobs, by now the unofficial skipper of the side, became hospital-bound with a virus infection, and such was his disappointment that he started talking about quitting the game and wanting to return home to his beloved 'Pooler'. I could understand his frustration and there were a number of us looking out of our Wellington hotel windows and watching the panes lashed by the rain who knew exactly how frustrated and disillusioned he was at that time. But there was the important matter of the third test to consider as well.

After our game against Auckland, where we quashed deserved local optimism by crushing the Auckland pack with a marvellous forward performance, we retired for a holiday in the Bay of Islands. The New Zealand selectors decided to drop Sid Going from the third test, and we had mixed thoughts about that. With Sid Going in the team, you knew exactly what kind of game to expect from the All Blacks. With the old campaigner and maestro out of the reckoning, the All Blacks would attempt to run at us in the three-quarters. It also meant that the All Blacks selectors had accepted that there was little point in taking the Lions pack up front, – a rare compliment to the 1977 Lions forwards. Even on our holiday break, however, the rain followed us around, and events such as trips, golf tournaments and outdoor pursuits remained very much on the 'Weather permitting' basis.

As we left for the islands we were joined by Clive Williams's replacement, Charlie Faulkner of Pontypool, who immediately showed the perspective of a man who had downed tools at breakfast to fly out to New Zealand.

'What kind of place is this Dundee like?' he asked, as we approached Dunedin.

Dunedin in the third test was some kind of place! The All Blacks went ahead in the game with a try from Ian Kirkpatrick after forty-five seconds. The Lions backs, myself included, chose that particular afternoon to show the worst possible form. I kicked and passed like a novice, gave my threes more problems than I gave the opposition and generally could do nothing right. Both Andy Irvine and I missed crucial kicks, and we ended up apologizing to the forwards and Terry Cobner. It was a game to forget, but this had been the one we knew we had to win. Our pack had once again played their hearts out; if they didn't feel like talking to the likes of me at the end of the third test, I could well understand why.

It was after the third test that I felt the worst pangs of

depression. The defeat had set us back; though I had to admit that the All Blacks, especially Graham Mourie, had tackled magnificently, we should have won with our forward dominance. I felt a failure as a captain and would willingly have given the responsibility to someone else at that stage. The thought of the homewardbound journey seemed an attractive proposition. By this time, too, a number of extra pressmen had arrived from Britain to give their opinion on what was going wrong and what we should have done, or could do, to put matters right. I say pressmen, but they were really friends: Barry John, Carwyn James and Mervyn Davies, who were now representing various journalistic organizations. All three had been highly critical of the Lions after watching them in Britain on television. Though their comments hurt a great deal, at this juncture of the tour I just had to accept that they were probably right.

Carwyn in particular had been unequivocal in his analysis of the team, and I suppose for me, his criticisms were that much more unpalatable because he was the man who had guided me for much of my career, and certainly had my wholehearted respect.

John Dawes was far more forthright when he heard of Carwyn's remarks. 'Who the hell is he?'

I'm sure that the remarks were well intentioned, but the climate that they created between the touring party and the press gang was unreal. John felt that he had been betrayed by his former team-mates and coach and the animosity resulted in a series of ugly affairs. The arrival of Messrs John, James and Davies merely served to inflame an already bitter war between the management and the other press members. What was far more disturbing was that the annoyance of the management at the way things were going came to the fore in other areas as well; not only clubs and New Zealand officials came in for unwarranted flak, but scores of children at various towns and playing fields as well. By the time the third test match had passed, and the scribes had again vented their wrath upon us for what was admittedly a poor performance, this really had become 'a bad news tour'.

There were three matches left before the last and final test. You did get a feeling of anti-climax as we approached the final test. I kept trying to convince myself that a drawn series in New Zealand wouldn't look at all bad on paper, and we could hardly put on as pathetic a show in the backs as we had at Dunedin. Even at this late stage, injuries were again disrupting our selection options. Charlie had joined us, and by the time we played North Auckland, Alun Lewis had also flown from home as a replacement for the desperately unlucky Brynmor Williams. We returned to winning ways against Thames Valley, North Auckland and the Bay of Plenty, but the cost of those games in terms of injury was great. Mike Gibson and Bruce Hay pulled hamstrings against the Bay of Plenty, J.J. Williams broke down during final preparations for the test and then two key members of the pack, Terry Cobner and Derek Quinnell, also withdrew. It was quite incredible. A day before the test match, the game where some measure of pride could be salvaged, we were forced more or less to pick a team with nearly half the touring party injured.

As it turned out, even without the comfort of having fit replacements on the bench, the Lions pack turned in another gargantuan performance. Hardly did the All Blacks take any possession at all in the first half and such was our dominance up front that New Zealand resorted to using three-man scrums against us. Yet we, the backs, failed to capitalize, though I must admit that the main part of the operation was to hoist high kicks against the New Zealand defence, and to go up on them early. The plan seemed to work. At half-time the Lions were in front by 9 points to 3 but the dividends on the scoreboard should have been more plentiful.

Then came the second half, which of all the rugby periods in New Zealand is the one I'd most willingly like to forget. Again the forwards were dominant, but when Bev Wilson kicked a goal and Doug Morgan failed to do the same for us, the All Blacks somehow, inexplicably, were within a score of levelling or even winning the game. We then made a hash of things, or, perhaps more accurately, I made a hash of things.

From a scrum the All Blacks hoisted a high kick. Going underneath it, I fielded it and my first thoughts were of a long driving kick into their territory. There was that need to keep them away from an attacking position. However the kick went towards Bill Osborne and he seized upon the chance to put more pressure on the Lions' line with another kick down into out twenty-two. Steve Fenwick got underneath this one and fed Peter Wheeler the hooker. Wheeler was tackled by Mourie, the ball went loose into Knight's hands and he went for the corner. They had won the series by three games to one and we had lost this one by a point. God, I felt sick!

The walk back to the changing room was filled with thoughts of wretchedness at having spent so much time and effort to see at least a share of success flitted away by a misdirected kick. I couldn't face my fellow Lions; neither could I face John Dawes, who had nearly seen his men bring about a certain amount of pride back into what had been a forgettable series.

As our jet left New Zealand soil a loud cheer of relief from the weary Lions signalled the end of the 1977 tour. As we headed for a brief stop and a game in the friendly Fijian Islands, some of us reflected on the reasons for the lost series and our failure to reach our full potential. It had already been dubbed as the 'bad news tour' and inevitably we started to look for excuses.

As a party we were an inexperienced group of players. Granted, there were those on board who had already travelled the world, but there were also a number who had hardly been weaned on the international stage, let alone on a long and prestigious tour.

If Gareth had been present in the third test, I think that his experience would have offered the Lions backs the time and composure to create openings from the un-limited opportunities offered to us by the forwards' dominance. We were also too late in recognizing the need for a forward general, and after the emergence of Terry Cobner as a natural pack leader, the difference was remarkable. At three-quarters we made far too many mistakes, and rarely set the world alight with penetrating running. In defence, despite some heroic tackling we needed the presence of Ray Gravell to knock down the powerful New Zealand centres.

The tour itself was far too long and the atrocious weather merely accentuated that fact. There were hotels that I would never visit again, and it was only after a confrontation with our management after the New Zealand Juniors game that, as players, we summoned up enough courage to complain about the food, which at times bordered on the miserly.

If it was an unhappy time, a great deal of that was our doing. The management over-reacted to criticism and, as a touring party, we became withdrawn and intro-spective. To those who still insist that there was too much revelry on the tour, my response is that there was no more than during the 1974 Lions tour; that tour was successful, and so little mention was made of parties and high jinks. I suspect too, that the relations between John Dawes and some of the press members before we arrived in New Zealand had not been amicable and the close proximity of Lions and press merely re-ignited old scores. A little more tolerance on both sides would have settled a great deal more than the early-morning slang-ing matches ever did.

And when all is said and done, I am well aware that, as a captain, I was a failure.

9

My Kind of Guy

Gareth is having his third rubdown of the weekend with the Welsh physio Gerry Lewis, Grav is explaining and half singing the latest Dafydd Iwan song to Steve Fenwick, who looks far more bewildered by 'this joker' from West Wales than he does trotting out to meet international opposition in a few minutes' time. I've gone through my pre-match rituals – a couple of bets on the horses, a look at the soccer highlights on 'Grandstand' – and I'm now sitting on a chair near the showers, going through the official programme, listening all the time and watching the others go through their own special forms of preparation.

The most nervous by far is Geoff Wheel, who changes as usual next door to me. 'Nothing in this Moss Keane is there, Phil? Nothing at all.' I wink at him, but my encouragement isn't enough, so off he goes to seek Charlie Faulkner's confirmation that there is nothing in the Keane fellow. Edwards is still hogging the rubdown bench, lying there wondering if he can snatch another ball at the end of this game. What on earth he does with all those footballs I'll never know. He must use them as fishing markers on the river Teifi.

'Phil, ask G.O. if I can have a game today?' It's a stock joke from Gerald, who like Steve appears to be unmoved by the drama that is continually building up outside the changing room and from within. I remember watching Gerald arrive at Stradey for one of those Llanelli–Cardiff spectaculars. He and Gareth and Barry had walked past our changing room with an air of confidence that sent our captain Norman Gale into a furious fit. 'Look at those three,' he snarled, 'think they're blinkin' chocolate, don't they, waving their Cambridge scarves about the place'. Gerald certainly had confidence, but it wasn't generated by his Oxbridge education nor his multitude of caps ... it was a presence of mind – he would do his best for club and country, but more than anything else he would enjoy himself.

Edwards has vacated the slab, and it's now the turn of Graham Price. Pricey's rubdown is painful to watch. Gerry Lewis, who probably needs a fortnight's vacation after every international, slowly turns Graham's upper torso into a glowing and flaming red mass. I've never ceased to wonder at the sight of this tower of a man, who goes through what must be more torment on the slab than he does under any New Zealand ruck.

J.P.R. is content to sit down and wonder about his 'attitude'. There are times when I think he's happy just knocking down men and emerging from tackles that have made the rest of us wince. There is nothing at all wrong with his attitude. Whatever he turns his attention to, he'll introduce an element of competitiveness to it. His namesake J.J. is still wondering whether he's been 'done' in his sale of tickets, sitting on the bench, pounds in one hand and small change in the other. If ever they need a new chancellor of the exchequer in Downing Street, J.J. is their man. Pensive and neurotic he may be about his finances, obviously a source of humorous bantering between us, but he's also a great friend to have in one's corner.

The other frugal spirit within the camp is Bobby Windsor, quietly rolling his own cigarettes in the corner, and contemplating the first put-in.

There is nervous excitement, a great deal of chatter, as the referee enters the room and beckons me outside to toss up with the opposing captain. It's a brief encounter and we both wish each other well, which is probably the most insincere remark of the afternoon. English referees are so precise ... 'It's 2.41 I shall call you in sixteen and a half minutes.' They may be the world's best time keepers, but generally they are very poor referees.

I may have come across a few referees in New Zealand and South Africa who have cheated, but the English attitude towards refereeing is all wrong. A number of them are under the impression that the players and crowd are there to appreciate their interpretation of the laws rather than a game of rugby football. Yet my favourite has always been Johnnie Johnson of England – hard, fair ... but with an open attitude toward a running game of rugby. I have nothing but admiration for his control. His countrymen should take note.

The singing can be heard for miles around. 'It makes you feel ten feet tall,' Jeff Young the Welsh hooker had told me before my first cap. He was wrong, it makes you tremble at the knee ... as a novice you don't quite recover from the incredible noise at the National Stadium for the first ten minutes.

John Dawes the coach has been in to check if everyone is all right. He's calm and collected. He will have already told me about the conditions out there, the wind, what time the sun will cause problems over the South Stand ... because I never go out on the pitch before a game, a superstition.

'We are going to lift them today, Benny,' shouts Charlie Faulkner, who fiddles around looking for something to do, since he'll have changed a quarter of an hour before everybody else. The game's honours came late for Charlie, and he savours every drop of the atmosphere. He won't let Wales down today ... he never does.

Suddenly, without warning, we are all alone and the time to go out has arrived. Hardly a word is spoken except by 'Wheelo' still investigating the merits of Moss Keane and 'Grav' jockeying for second-out-on-the-field position.

'OK,' I tell them, 'let's go out and do it.' More often than not they did.

The foresight of the Welsh rugby establishment in

founding the squad system had produced massive dividends. It has become the premier club team in Wales and such is the camaraderie between fellow members that I've often felt that I've come to know players from other clubs as well as I know my own Llanelli colleagues. No matter how England organize their squads and regional trials, they will always be troubled by the geographical distances between the strongholds of rugby in the North and the West. However the Welsh system also has its drawbacks, because the player will invariably find that between club matches and training commitments, and on top of that calls to the squad sessions on Thursdays and Sundays, there is barely time for anything else. Add to that the continual presence of the rugby press with their insatiable readers, the Welsh player often has to disengage himself from all that is happening around him in order to concentrate on the most important matter – beating the opposition.

I've known players to collapse mentally from the strain of it all: the ticket-seekers, the 'long-lost friends', reporters, and the 'heavies'. It is all part of the Welsh rugby mania, that seems to gain more momentum with each international. Gradually you learn to live with it, and grow wise because of it. Inside the Welsh camp itself, there are few who would like to see any of the paranoic build-up change. I for one have missed it all, and during the last couple of years before retiring I had a hankering for a return to the international arena.

It's much the same on a British Lions tour or a Barbarian trip. Friendships are made that will last a lifetime and these are welded together because at one stage there has been a common bond.

Though the Barbarians and the British Lions attract the attention and obviously are the prestigious tours, there is no doubt in my mind that the most enjoyable of the touring companies is that of the Crawshay fifteen. Selected from the senior clubs in Wales, it provides the player with an escape route to the West Country, France and North Wales. Of course, any player will give com-

mitment to a game but somehow, because of the convivial atmosphere created by the likes of the organizers
Arthur Rees, Viv Jenkins and Neville Walsh, I've always
been delighted to accept their invitations. Their attitude
is that the player comes first and the needs of the
committee come second. They are a joyful company.

For someone like me, so attached to home and the
little square acre that is Felinfoel, having people around
that were likeable and understanding was vitally important. I make no excuse for the fact that I am more of a
home-bird than most, though the *hiraeth* has been to my
detriment at crucial stages in my rugby career.

In gratitude to the people and the players that I've
had the pleasure of meeting and playing with and
against, I would like to dwell on the merits of the best of
them. Some may consider this an introspective exercise,
but at least it may satisfy those who continually ask me
to name the best outside-half, centre or flanker that I've
ever played with or against. Indeed, if I had been given a
pound for every time that I've been asked that question
in the smoke-filled halls of Wales, I could in all probability have saved the Duport steelworks in Llanelli.

'Can Mr Phil Bennett name the best outside-half he's
ever played with or against?' The questioner sits down
and no matter whom I will eventually choose it won't be
to the liking of him or his friends, since they've already
decided upon the answer themselves.

'David Watkins of Newport,' I might answer and I can
imagine hearing mutterings at the back of 'what a load
of rubbish' before I have sat down.

So, to satisfy the experts of the back stalls, I would like
to indulge in a feast of selection ponderables. I make no
apologies for selecting a team that would be suited to my
kind of rugby, a team equipped to win sufficient ball in
the set pieces and with the talent behind to execute accurately and attractively. The purists may question the
motives behind certain choices and emphasize that others
were technically better than my selections. I have no
arguments with such logic ... that is their prerogative.

J.P.R. Williams was not the most complete full-back that I've ever seen on a rugby field, nor was he the fastest; but would anyone argue that he was not the best? A mountain of courage to have behind any three-quarters line, his call for a high ball when Hannibal's elephants were about to descend upon him went unchallenged. The highest compliment that one can pay a full-back is to approach a game knowing that a misdirected kick into his territory will probably be punished with great severity. You would always kick well away from J.P.R., since his intuitive flair for running at the opposition was often far more telling than a long line-kick out of defence. Terry Price of Llanelli was the most gifted of full-backs that I have played with, but alas we rarely saw the best of him in a Welsh jersey. His talent was squandered for reasons best known to himself but Terry, much in the same way as J.P.R., could win a game by his own influence and deeds. Andy Irvine was another exceptional player who was blessed with the speed of a wing and the positional sense of a chess player. Because of our failure as a three-quarter unit in New Zealand in 1977, he enhanced his reputation as a player of considerable individual merit and was one of our few successes behind the scrum. Fergie McCormick of New Zealand is another I would rank as from the top drawer. However, when the merits of each player are assessed, the best criterion often is to consider the virtues of a player when matters are going against the tide – and in rough waters I cannot think of a better lifesaver than J.P.R.

A decade of witnessing and participating in international rugby has left me with wondrous tales to relate about dazzling sidesteps and swerves, of great passers of the ball and the quickness of individual minds. To select a quartet of individuals and two half-backs who should rank as the cream of ten years is an invidious task, and some may think that my sights should no be so parochial when choosing a pair of half-backs. But I'm sure that they would start sending for the white coats unless my final selection honoured those two 'Kardiff' comics –

Barry and Gareth. Because of their outstanding success on the 1971 Lions tour and for the Welsh team in the early seventies, many people tend to forget that it took some time for this durable unit to settle into such a smooth and effective combination. Eventually the arrogance, and I use that word kindly, of the two moulded as fine a combination as the Welsh supporter is likely to see. It all looked so intuitive at times, the slight wheel of the scrum, Edwards going to the short side, haltering for a moment and then sending a reverse-spin pass to a waiting John who had stood there for some time wondering why 'Gwauncaegurwen' had gone blind in the first place. It still puzzles a number of people why it took so long to discover Barry's ability as a goal-kicker. I'm not at all sure whether J.P.R. and Gareth enjoyed being displaced by The King, but there was no doubting the regal instep once it got going.

I would insist on including the John and Edwards combination as a pair, since there were others, of course, who might rival them for selection as individuals. The threat of Sid Going has been a constant worry for all British teams. When people are delegated the responsibility of shepherding one man, that again is a mark of respect. Derek Quinnell will tell you all about Sid Going, and such was the influence of his presence in the New Zealand team against the Lions in 1977 that we resorted to spreading rumours that he was the weak link in their attacking manoeuvres, in the forlorn hope that the All Black selectors might drop him. New Zealand supporters consider him supreme, but the vintage Edwards in his latter seasons was a delight to watch. Everything was done with economy of effort but with maximum impact. The long low kicks could destroy opposing packs, the sheer force of speed and strength would make a try from a five-yard scrum inevitable, and to be at the end of that magnificent pass gave you enough time to call a different three-quarter move if the necessity arose. How we missed him in New Zealand!

The challengers to Barry John are fewer in number.

137

Whereas arguments could rage over the relative merits of Gareth against the talents of the Goings, De Villiers and the Catchpoles of the rugby world, I have yet to see an outside-half dominate a team's performance as much as Barry. His reading of situations only slightly surpassed his native cunning. Some have referred to his ability to 'ghost' through defences with a swivel of the hips, and that was an important skill. His confidence also allowed him to wait for the opponent to hesitate momentarily and, after showing him the ball, John had granted himself a half-yard licence to kill. Barry John complemented Gareth's ability at the base of the scrum and, I have no doubt that Barry would agree, Edwards could transpose a bit character into a lead part. Kirton of Otago and McGann of Ireland were two number tens that I admired greatly. Both possessed natural flair; so did Tony Ward, who replaced Barry McGann. The latter never forgot that rugby was primarily an enjoyable pastime and, though his waistline threw doubts on his credibility as a runner, there was little to question about his kicking ability.

Selecting the three-quarters presents a multiplicity of problems. It is at this stage that I may have to indulge in a little parochialism once again. The choice of Gerald Davies will hardly surprise anyone, though I would advocate J.J. Williams as a close second. J.J. suffered as a player because of his selection on the left wing for Wales. I know that he was disappointed when after Gerald's departure from the Welsh team the selectors insisted on keeping him on the left. He was undoubtedly at his peak, the fastest wing in the world, and there were few who could compete with his work rate. Bobby Windsor the Welsh hooker never ceased to be amazed at J.J.'s speed in being first to the line-out ... no matter where play had been. It was J.J.'s misfortune that Gerald was around when it came to selection. Ball in hand, with two yards to spare, a dip of the shoulders and a scampering of feet, Gerald could break, into Fort Knox. Perhaps our over-indulgence in the Welsh team in the use of the crash ball limited Gerald's chances of further exploits; in retrospect several of us responsible for this tactic, including myself, would have to plead guilty. Gerald was a match winner of exceptional quality, unsurpassed in attacking ability and a menace if you had to face him. People held their breath when 'Reames' was given the ball ... and few have been given that accolade.

On the left, the competition is even more intense. Since I believe that the right was J.J.'s best position I am reluctant to place him in contention. Probably the most logical method of deciding who to nominate is to consider the one you least liked to oppose. David Duckham with those long striding legs, the change of pace and the massive side-step, was a player of whom we didn't see enough, since he was a victim of an uneasy three-quarter combination in the English squad. John Bevan of Wales had the strength of a prop and the determination of a commando; though not blessed with the subtler skills, he was a player who had to be placed on the deck or the consequences would have to be paid. Grant Batty of New Zealand, an aggressive individual, had a calm conciseness about him that lulled the opposition into a false sense of security. Behind the bristling moustache there was a great will to succeed, and an even greater determination not to be intimidated. Maurice Richards of Wales is another winger of exceptional quality who comes to mind. Sadly, he left for the Northern code, by his own invitation, and rugby in the Welsh amateur ranks was that much poorer for his decision. All these players were endowed with skills that could inspire others to greater deeds. However, if Gerald on the right wing could threaten the most efficient of defences so could another right-winger, Bryan Williams of New Zealand. He possessed a side-step and a turn of speed that would often leave his man for dead. He too suffered from insufficient service from his three-quarters but, given room and quick delivery of the ball, Bryan – who had pistons for legs – was a man that everybody hated to tackle. I'd have him in any selected team, though he was a 'rightie'.

The centres have to combine flair, technique, attacking and defensive potential; centre is a position that demands all the skills, and rarely in one man does one find everything that is required. The exception was Mike Gibson of Ireland. Not only did he have the pace to break both on the inside and the outside of his man, but he had sufficient awareness of the frailties of his colleagues to compensate for them on his own. During the lean periods for Ireland, he was the one player who had to be watched lest he turned the tide of matters on his own. His intuition led him to the most penetrating of support positions and he was no mean kicker of the ball either.

Several people saw the combination of John Dawes and Mike Gibson as the ideal collaboration of skills. They were indeed a marvellous force to have in the middle of the 1971 Lions backs but, as much as I admired 'Sid' for his distribution, and most of all for his captaincy, there have been others who have to my mind been slightly superior as running three-quarters.

Ian MacRae of New Zealand was; Maso of France had that Gallic flair of speed and magnetic hands; Jock Turner of Scotland was a complete and gifted footballer. There is, however, one player who commanded the attention of Ray Gravell and Roy Bergiers, two not inconsiderable tacklers, when they faced up to him during a Llanelli tour of South Africa – Jogi Jansen. He was the biggest centre I've ever seen; not only that, he was fast and agile. It was both terrifying and exciting to watch him stir into action, taking three men out of the game and delivering a score-winning pass to his wing. Bryan Williams scored four tries for the World fifteen playing outside Jansen, and I only wish that we had had the opportunity of seeing Jogi in full stride on the fields of Wales.

Now it may be a bit presumptuous of me to deal with forward selection, since I've been told in no uncertain manner at club level to mind my own business when such matters are discussed. If I offend those who are blessed with the knowledge of the mischievous deeds that are committed in the 'inner sanctum' of the game, then I can only claim political asylum in the three-quarter symposiums. I will be scorned by the purists for having chosen two tight-head forwards as props. They are simply the two best front-row forwards I have seen and since one is from New Zealand, where they are far more liberal when choosing between tight and loose, I make no apologies. The New Zealander, Ken Gray, had enormous strength; whereas the front-row club may stress the technique of Ray McLoughlin, I only wish they had been there to witness what Mr Gray did to the Welsh scrummaging on that fateful 1969 tour. He simply destroyed and toyed with the Welsh challenge.

On the other side, against the challenges of the likes of Hopkinson of New Zealand, Scholey of France, Scotland's 'Mighty Mouse', Marais of South Africa and Cotton of England, I have chosen Graham Price of Wales.

He is a product of the Pontypool school, and the cornerstone of the latterday improvement in the Welsh scrum. The New Zealanders were prepared to concede to him, and as yet I have seen no one to challenge his rightful position in a World fifteen. Apart from his ability in the set-pieces he demonstrated in the most startling fashion possible at his Parc des Princes debut that he's quite a sprinter.

To complete the front row, the merits of the Welsh hookers Norman Gale and Bobby Windsor make it difficult to cast an objective eye on the matter. Ken Kennedy of Ireland, Peter Wheeler and John Pullin of England are three born with a competitive spirit that is uncompromising and so essential for that most vulnerable of positions. However, in a game that requires all eight men to produce a shove in order to disrupt the opposition's possession, I return to that Welsh tour of 1969 and opt for Bruce McLeod of New Zealand. The New

141

Zealand's front row during that tour demoralized the Welsh ranks, and McLeod as much as anyone denied the Welsh any positive ball at all.

There have been two world rugby giants that I've admired and it has been my privilege to meet. One was the legendary Don Clarke, who was as impressive a man as I'd wanted him to be, and the other was 'Pinetree' Meads. I didn't play against Meads, but saw enough of this massive man to know no team of any substantial merit would be complete without his inclusion. Again he was a member of the All Black pack that lowered the 1969 Dragon. To complement the support, strength and tenacity of Colin Meads, it would be wise to opt for a man capable of the two-handed catch in the line-out, someone who could deliver the ball to the scrum-half with the minimum of interference and in the quickest of time. There is no greater an admirer of the ability of Willie John McBride, Delme Thomas or Gordon Brown than I; they were all world-class forwards; with a battery of worthy challengers to contest them – Beaumont of England, Whiting of New Zealand and John Williams of South Africa – the choice of another lock is complicated by the immense amount of talent available. So it will surprise the pundits that I would eventually decide upon a man who was not a 'lock' specialist, a man who openly professed not to like the position at all. To my mind, however, there have been few lock-forwards to match the ball-winning ability of Walter Spanghero. Apart from his height advantage he was also as elusive as any three-quarter when breaking from the set-pieces. The French didn't recover until this year after his disappearance from the scene, which proves what an influential factor he was in the make-up of their national fifteen. I should state that the two flankers in any rugby team of this quality, or in any national fifteen, should complement each other. The options open to the selectors are to choose either a ball-carrier and a ball-winner, or an attacker and a defender. This theoretical type of selection has been the dominant theme in the Welsh selections of recent years – John Taylor and Dai Morris, Terry Cobner and Jeff Squire are two combinations which illustrate the effectiveness of having dual forces to call upon. So, with this in mind, I have chosen Peter Greyling of South Africa and Grahame Mourie of New Zealand. Greyling is such a powerful man coming away from the line-out, a frightening prospect for any outside half, and I know better than most that the defensive qualities of Graham Mourie are second to none. Added to that, Graham has that uncanny talent of being in the right place at all times, whether it be destroying the opposing side's attacking movement or generating a counter-attack on his own. There are those who extol the virtues of Jan Ellis of South Africa, but my appreciation of Jan Ellis, good though he was, is influenced by not having seen him in his prime.

Jean-Pierre Rives and Skrela were undoubtedly the most potent back-row force in European rugby towards the end of the seventies. It was unfortunate that the French adopted such a tight game during this time, forbidding these two to express themselves fully. Jean-Pierre, however, succeeded at times in creating fluidity even in the restrictive practices of a non-running game; his support play, combined with relentness energy, made him an invaluable asset of that French connection. There have been others of course who have accredited themselves superbly. I have always admired Tony Neary of England and thanked the England selectors for ignoring him so often against Wales. Terry Cobner and John Taylor of Wales turned in masterful performances, and my debt to Terry Cobner knows no bounds.

I do, however, without reservation select another Welshman as the final piece of this fantastic jigsaw. According to no less a person then Colin Meads, Mervyn Davies played a more than significant part in winning the 1971 test series in New Zealand for the Lions. His courage bordered on the manic, his pace around the field for such a large fellow was incredible and his work rate was quite extraordinary. As I've already stated elsewhere, he would undoubtedly have led the 1977 Lions, and the game in the British Isles could not have honoured a more worthy recipient than Swerv, if he had been fit.

There are scores of people that I haven't mentioned whom many would regard as contenders of any World fifteen of the last decade. Having looked at and questioned my own choice, I would be inclined to hesitate before entering into any further discussion on the subject lest I change my opinion. However, I do feel that having started out on the premise that the emphasis should have been on an attacking side I don't think my final selection that follows would have disappointed many. I'm sure they would have delighted millions. Here is my choice:

J.P.R. Williams (Wales); B. Williams (New Zealand); C.M.H. Gibson (Ireland); J. Jansen (South Africa); T.G.R. Davies (Wales); B. John (Wales); G.O. Edwards (Wales); K. Gray (New Zealand); B. McLeod (New Zealand); G. Price (Wales); C. Meads (New Zealand); W. Spanghero (France); P. Greyling (South Africa); G. Mourie (New Zealand); T. M. Davies (Wales).

My inclination towards Welsh players is a natural one, since the last decade in the northern hemisphere has been dominated by Wales in the home international championship. There are, perhaps, a few selections that might be questioned in the bars of Auckland and Wellington.

It is a point worth noting that whereas the home countries might play four or even five representative matches against different oppositions in a few months, the All Blacks, the Australians and, to a much greater degree, the Springboks, have barren periods of international engagements. Perhaps then as a tribute to those who have been fortunate enough to participate in this 'golden era' for Wales, I may be allowed to nominate the best representative fifteen from the Principality.

What say the pundits to this selection!

J.P.R. Williams (Bridgend); T.G.R. Davies (Cardiff); John Dawes, captain (London Welsh); Ray Gravell (Llanelli); Maurice Richards (Cardiff); Barry John (Cardiff); Gareth Edwards (Cardiff); Denzil Williams (Ebbw Vale); Norman Gale (Llanelli); Graham Price (Pontypool); Brian Price (Newport); Geoff Wheel (Swansea); Terry Cobner (Pontypool); John Taylor (London Welsh); Mervyn Davies (London Welsh).

There are omissions that will raise eyebrows and down glasses, but it is a team full of potential and try-scoring ability. Obviously there are those who would argue the case for Steve Fenwick of Bridgend, J.J. of Llanelli, Arthur Lewis of Ebbw Vale, Bobby Windsor of Ponty-pool, Dai Morris of Neath or Derek Quinnell of Llanelli. I mean no disrespect to these players or their supporters. I've been proud to have known them all, and without them the last ten years would have been a lean time.

Geoff Wheel trots off the Arms Park, his shirt stained by the rigours of the afternoon battle, and puts a hand on Charlie Faulkner's shoulder.

'Told you see, Charlie, nothing in that Moss Keane, was there!'

10

Paying My Round

The way some of those fellas up in London go on about Welsh rugby-players being treated like lords in the valleys sometimes convinces the uninitiated that life for a member of the Welsh rugby squad is a bed of roses. The gossip-mongers sometimes give the impression that a player who has scored a try on a Saturday only has to click his fingers on a Monday morning and any number of job offers will arrive on his desk or through the front door. When Barry became a superstar shortly before his retirement such rumours became even more convincing. Nobody bemoans Barry's success as an entrepreneur of his own talents, but there were, and still are, a number of international rugby players in Wales who have seen the other side of the coin. I remember on several occasions sitting in the Welsh dressing room reading the various job descriptions of some of my colleagues, knowing full well that the individual concerned, rather than being an engineer, construction worker or teacher, was simply unemployed. Even Barry had worrying moments wondering whether he was going to find the right sort of work that would enable him to carry on with his rugby career.

My own career would confound any Job Centre manager. When Coleshill Secondary School saw fit to release me to the big world outside at the age of fifteen, there was little alternative than to sign on with that big provider of wage packets, the Klondyke steelworks. It was of course my first taste of reality and, for a mere adolescent, a grim introduction. Twelve months later the

146

steelworks went into a slight slump and made me redundant; in a two-horse factory town I turned to the other employer, British Leyland. I spent two years there where the money was good and life as a machine operator was quite uncomplicated. Again the cards came, and with them the redundancy notice. The steelworks had recovered from its economic crisis by this time so I signed up again, knowing full well that the 'last in, first out' motto was very much the observed creed. After a couple of years I started looking around for an outside job, since the hours and the environment of the old Klondyke was neither doing my health nor my bank balance much good. I had some old Welsh social stigma at the back of my mind that I could do a bit better, though the lads at the steelworks were great friends and marvellous company. In fact I think that my gaffer at the works, Eric MacVicar, always kept one eye on the Llanelli fixture list and training nights before working out young Mr Bennett's work-sheets. Mind you, if Llanelli had lost on the Saturday, and thank goodness that was a fairly rare occurrence those days, life on the Klondyke floor could be pretty miserable. It was during those days that I realized that the Welsh have been given licence to criticize each other, but let a stranger say the same things about them, and he'll be quickly informed of the consequences. The Klondyke was the bastion of Llanelli rugby supporters, and I don't recall many Swansea people working there. There may have been a few, but they kept quiet about it.

I was then offered a job as an oil company representative, which sounds very grand indeed. The boys at the steelworks chipped in and gave me a briefcase as a going-away present. The young executive was also given a car. It all sounded too good to be true and, as I started on my first day, I had the sense of expectation of a young schoolboy in a new pair of trousers. The job lasted four days! I quickly realized that I was no more than a glorified bad-debt collector. A rather pushy area manager forced me into collecting a payment from a friend of mine who had promised to pay a bill after receiving a load of goods. I was forced to sit with my manager in my friend's front room awaiting his return. It was all too embarrassing, and I chucked in the job there and then.

'What happened to the car that went with the job then, Phil?' asked an inquisitive Edwards as we were changing in the Welsh dressing room.

'I had to give it back,' I replied.

'Four days!' Edwards couldn't control his laughter and I suspect that half of the Arms Park crowd knew about my four-day oil mogul job by the end of the afternoon.

Back I went to the steelworks feeling very sheepish about the briefcase. The welcome was one of shaking but smiling heads. But the third visit to the steelworks had the inevitable conclusion ... after a little less than two years I was again made redundant. That two-year period of stability was by our standards an economic boom for the Bennett family, which had by this time already welcomed Steven into the world.

Redundancy from the furnaces left me with little alternative but to seek the well-worn track back to British Leyland. The choice of jobs was extremely limited and I ended up keeping a line of bonus-seeking ladies supplied with tubes. The pace was non-stop, and whatever you were, Welsh outside-half or Prince of Wales, it didn't matter – if the tubes weren't there, they'd call you everything under the sun. Looking back, I suppose it was quite funny. On Saturday you'd be cheered on by thousands, watched by millions, interviewed on Grandstand ... and on Monday reality dawned with a shrieking 'Where's my bloody tubes, Mr Bennett!'

I left after thirteen days, feeling quite depressed and despondent. Fortunately along came two dear friends, Leon Lyons and Don Williams, who offered me a job handling wooden props on a mining construction site. I knew at the time there wasn't much work for me to do there, and what little there was ended up being done by Tom Long, a delightful Irishman.

'Don't you dirty those pretty little hands of yours, my little Phil,' he kept shouting, and between Tom's protective and goodly nature and the generosity of Leon and Don, I kept my head above water for three months until something else came along.

I was answering just about every job advert that appeared in the local press. Then, luckily Courage Breweries, prompted by Arwyn Edmunds and Dai Rowland, two highly influential local characters, came along and offered me a sales rep post in West Wales. Just before taking up the post there was a slight problem. Three days after I was due to finish with the construction site Wales were due to go on a short tour of Japan, and Pat and I spent many an hour working out how and if I could afford to go with them. Along came that generous man Don Williams again; he insisted that I should qualify for a month's wages, though I wasn't officially on his payroll. It was a fantastic gesture, one which I shall treasure for the rest of my life.

After returning from Japan, I started with Courage, travelling up and down the west Wales valleys and stopping at clubs and pubs. Needless to say, in a very short time indeed I had a bit of a weight problem ... though I liked the work well enough, the hospitality offered by clients and customers was at times a little over-generous. Besides, I'm an able procrastinator, without the help of others.

Eventually I decided to open a sports shop in Llanelli, again with the help of a friend with financial backing. We were able to do what so many sportsmen have done, that is to apply some of their knowledge in order to made ends meet. Even this enterprise has been dogged by the lack of prosperity in the South Wales region, and the closure of the Klondyke. So the future may well find me wheeling tubes to the conveyor belt again. God, I hope not!

My reason for mentioning that chronology of disastrous job sequences is merely to emphasize that the Welsh international rugby player is by no means offered a golden spoon to feed from. The opposite is far closer to the truth. There are those who have been fortunate enough to land good jobs during their playing careers but even they find that if the sales returns at the end of the month aren't up to scratch, it doesn't matter how many stand tickets you can cadge for the managing director – you are out on your neck!

Inevitably during the periods of doubt about making a go of any of the jobs that I've had, a knock would come on the door, and a man with a tempting cheque book and a broad Northern accent would be escorted into the front room. There were times that I was hard pressed to refuse rugby league offers for reasons that are fairly obvious when you consider my job prospects. I bear no grudge or malice towards any player who has 'gone North,' but somehow the thought of living away from my little neck of the woods deterred me from signing. The amounts mentioned seemed colossal: even in my last playing season I was offered a £30,000 plus figure to turn professional for three years ... and they didn't even want me to live in the North. I have never turned away a rugby league scout from our house, and at times they've even asked for my opinion of prospective clients of theirs. In my dealings with them I have always found them to be warmhearted and courteous, and not, I believe, because of the obvious motive.

Even after years of their trying to persuade me to hang my boots in Warrington or St Helens, my attitude hasn't changed. Some players are ideally suited for the Northern code, I think especially of John Bevan, Roy Mathias and Glyn Shaw, who all sought the riches of the professional game. I have doubts about my own suitability: taking those bone-shattering tackles Sunday after Sunday – it sounds like too much hard work. I remember the first approach quite well. It was in my first season with Llanelli and one of the clubs sent a man called Don Vine to the house. Don was about six foot three in height, with gnarled features and the scars of a career in the league game. To be perfectly honest, he frightened me stiff, and convinced me that life would be far healthier in the rosy confines of Welsh rugby football.

Since that first carrot was dangled in front of me, and I think the sum was something approaching £10,000, I've watched the scouts not only come for me but other Llanelli players as well. They seem to have a good network of informants and it always surprised me to see them swarm for a man who had just been made unemployed. That is possibly the reason that they kept me under a fair amount of surveillance! It would have been nice to forget all the financial worries just by signing on the line, but somehow the attachment to Wales and loyalty to the village and the Llanelli area pricked my conscience just at the right moment. Even the establishment of a rugby league club at Cardiff hasn't whetted my appetite. I'm simply not keen on the game.

Mind, there have been a lot of times when certain events would have taxed even the most loyal of rugby union devotees. Perhaps the time is approaching for us to examine not only our coaching methods – woefully exposed at the Arms Park by the All Blacks in the WRU centenary year – but also our attitude towards players who have achieved international status and are thus constantly in demand. During the months of January, February and March, the player hardly has a spare moment to himself. On the Monday it's usually an evening with the club's physiotherapist recovering from a Saturday injury. Tuesday is the club's training night; Wednesday usually finds a club or charity game filling the time; Thursday is either the WRU run-out or a couple of hours road-running, and invariably the weekdays end with a function. In Wales the demands during the weekends are strenuous, with club matches followed on the Sunday by work-outs at the Afan Lido with the rest of the squad. Added to this list were my committee meetings and selection nights with Llanelli. The spectator who turns up on a Wednesday night or Saturday afternoon expects the very peak of the individual's performance. It's a demand that is not always satisfied ... simply because the player is tired or, perhaps, even bored with rugby. There is hardly any rest at all for the international who is fortunate to be selected for a Lions tour. It is a great honour to be picked for the Lions, but after a hard season – especially so since the fixture card of a Welsh rugby club calls on the individual to play in excess of forty games on top of his commitments to his country – it's easy to understand why form fluctuates. We devised a system at Llanelli where those selected for Wales on the Saturday would not be selected for the club on the previous Saturday. It worked well, since it not only gave the person a chance to freshen up his attitude, but also gave some of the younger players in the club a chance to blood their talents. But we were fortunate in Llanelli to have adequate reserves. In a club that may only have one international or squad member, the committee will always expect that player to give of his best in every game; the player, loyal to his club, doesn't want to be seen to be difficult. It is up to the committee to protect such players by exercising their wisdom in knowing when a player is overcommitting himself to the game. But you'll always get the boys from the old brigade who say that, in their days, playing for the club and then playing for Wales was not unduly strenuous, in fact was most welcome. But the introduction of the squad system and its twice weekly get-togethers has made extra demands on the players, and I know that some rugby players spend more time involved with their sport than many a full-time soccer player does with his.

Though rugby football is an amateur game, certain aspects in its administration should be revised immediately. Too many of our committees and bureaucrats are hiding behind the amateur image and have never listened to the demands or even considered the welfare of their players. The WRU, for all the well-orchestrated trumpet-blowing in their centenary year, have been at times outrageously ignorant of the players' needs.

I can remember going to Twickenham one year. The party, as usual, assembled on the Friday evening for a visit to a London show. Now that might sound like a very comfortable way of spending an evening in the West End, but you may perhaps understand the apprehension I was feeling when I tell you that on the three previous visits to Twickenham, the WRU had booked us in to see the 'Black and White Minstrel Show'. On this particular occasion there had been a change in the itinerary.

'Where are we going this year then?' I asked one of the committee men.

'Babes in the Wood!' came the reply.

I was absolutely staggered. There were some twenty grown men who were about to go to battle for their country at Twickenham, and here we were, surrounded by kids watching a pantomime! I can even remember the kindly physio Gerry Lewis handing out choc ices at half-time. Needless to say there had to be some explanation for the choice of entertainment, and so a few of us went looking for Bill Clement of the WRU. The answer was more entertaining than the panto.

'What you don't realize is that you have to book these shows well in advance, and, when we ring up, the best ones are always full.'

And that reply came from a man who knew six years in advance when Wales were playing at Twickenham.

It also took the WRU nearly a century to acknowledge that players might be married. On the Saturday night after one international in Cardiff, there were scenes in some of the players' bedrooms that were straight out of a Rix farce. The WRU had invited the players' wives to the after-match dance, but expected the individual players to find accommodation for their wives. Anybody who has ever tried to get a room in Cardiff on an international weekend knows what an impossible task that is, and so quite naturally you had to improvise. So, on the Saturday, Gareth and his wife Maureen, together with Pat and myself, or it might be J.J. and his wife, would toss up to see who could have first use of the bathroom as changing quarters. With the Edwards tucked in one single bed and the Bennetts in another, the morning-coffee porter at the Angel Hotel had a tall story to tell his colleagues downstairs. Even more ridiculous was the situation, where the new cap would sleep in the bath so that the more seasoned international could share a bed with his wife in the adjoining room. That has all changed, fortunately, and now the wives are invited to stay with their husbands on Saturday night. But it took the WRU until the early seventies to recognize the injustice of it all.

As players we might have won a bit of a concession at the Angel Hotel – but outside Wales we might as well be in the Dark Ages. On one Twickenham trip, the wives had gone to London by train and the English players' wives had gone to a lot of trouble to entertain them – it would have been too much to ask the WRU to look after them. Since the official coach was half empty for the return journey to Wales, a few of us asked the chairman of the selectors, Cliff Jones, if the wives could travel with us on the team coach rather than catch a train. Not an unreasonable request, since the officials and their wives had a bus of their own. Permission was granted.

We had a lunch stop scheduled at Swindon and before going into the restaurant I again asked Cliff if it would be OK if Pat and the other wives could accompany us.

'Fine,' said Cliff, and he said it with good grace.

A fortnight later I received a bill from the Welsh Rugby Union for a £3.58 lunch! I sent them a cheque. A fortnight later we were playing Scotland in Cardiff. On the Sunday we were hemmed in by snow and in order to get back to work I had to fork out £12 for a train ticket. My car, which had been driven by friends, was still stuck in a Cardiff multistorey car park and so during the week I again had to pay for an extra train journey to go and get it. So, what did all that little lot cost me? I wonder what the reaction would have been at the Welsh HQ if I'd handed in a bill for all those extra expenses. £3.58 for lunch, my foot!

It seems that the *cardi* attitude towards the players' welfare reflects committees across the border as well. When we were travelling around New Zealand in 1977 we heard about the arrangements for the Queen's Jubilee

154

Lions v. Barbarians match at Twickenham. It was to be a grand occasion and the Barbarians committee, probably with the best intentions in the world, had picked a very strong fifteen to face the Lions. I must admit that we were a bit surprised to find that for such a unique event in British rugby they had seen fit to pick the French back-row, but that made us even more determined to do well. We also had to show the British public that we weren't the failures that we'd been dubbed after losing the tèst series. It was to be a grand reunion and the Four Home Unions Committee told us that we'd be housed in the Hilton. This was indeed a welcome departure. However, we were also told that wives wouldn't be allowed to join us until the morning of the match. Again that enforced Victorian celibacy. I simply couldn't understand why our wives couldn't be allowed to travel to London with us. I've no doubt that some sports psychiatrist somewhere had convinced the powers-that-be that being with your wife before an important match tends to distract. The psychiatrists of this world would be better employed changing a few attitudes at the top. Or is it simply a case of penny-pinching? Whatever the reason or excuse, it angered us.

So quite bluntly, we sent a message to London to tell them that unless the wives and girlfriends could enjoy a full weekend in London, we simply wouldn't play.

Our demands were met, but not in full. Instead of wallowing in the luxury of the London Hilton, the committee changed the booking and we spent the weekend in suburban surroundings at the Star and Garter Hotel in Richmond. Grateful for small mercies, we consented to play. I just wonder how much money was taken at the gate for that match, and whether the Jubilee funds would have been that much worse off if the Lions and the Barbarians, and their wives, had been housed in the Hilton. It was all so characteristic of the inconsiderate attitude of the rugby godfathers. It really doesn't surprise me to hear of rugby union officials going to sleep during internationals and waking up at the end asking what the score is.

It isn't that the player wants to be paid or compensated in any way by financial inducements. It is a matter quite simply of showing consideration and giving the individual his just rewards. I remember castigating the Llanelli committee for not having visited an international player in hospital who had just broken his leg playing for the club. He had been there for two days before any of the club's administrators had bothered to check up on his condition. I would go so far as to suggest to many clubs that they must wake up to the realities of the twentieth century. If they demand the time and the energy of their players to turn up twice a week for training as well as the Saturday game, then the players should be treated with a little respect.

Carwyn showed the way to Llanelli by considering each individual as a person. He knew that every player was motivated by different factors, he knew that each player came from a different background, and he went to great pains to show to each member of the Llanelli squad that he cared for his well-being. I know that to quite a few of the Llanelli committee his attitude was considered ridiculous and far-fetched. But the players greatly appreciated his concern and it was little wonder that on the Saturday we were willing to give our best.

Rugby football is still an amateur game, yet its future is threatened by factors that have been introduced by the professional media. To say that the game is an amateur sport in Wales or New Zealand is simply ignoring the reality of the situation. Hundreds of journalists, pundits and technicians make a living out of the game, yet, with admirable piety, they are the very people who insist on the amateur status. We have seen sponsorship enter the game, from everything from slaughterhouses to paint manufacturers, and all of them help to keep the coffers brimming. During the seventies, breweries, soft drinks and razor blade companies have entered the arena so that they can benefit from the odd radio mention or accidental shot on television of their hoardings at the various grounds. Small children are ordered not to sit in front of the touch-line advertisements, and administrators find themselves at a loss trying to choose which particular pre-match reception they should endorse.

The Welsh Rugby Union centenary has witnessed a small industrial revolution in rugby memorabilia: scarves, books, mugs, ties, each one of them bearing the crest of the union. Yet this is the same union which until very recently debated about the introduction of sponsorship, and in some quarters denied the right of the rugby league man, a true professional, to enter and enjoy the welcome of his former union club and colleagues. The matches played at the Arms Park during the season have been stage-managed with all the precision of a military tattoo and the public have responded by turning up in their thousands. And why shouldn't they? It has been a marvellous celebration. Yet there is so much hypocrisy about. The WRU member who will accept his token gift of special wine from a Cardiff dealer or the various 'appreciation' gestures from clubs and organizations, is the same man that in committee will deny the player even the most trivial of considerations. I would be the last to criticize the administrator for accepting mugs, tankards and plaques; but let there be consistency. The time will come when compensation will have to be paid to the players involved in long tours and endless practice sessions. Will the administrators throw up their arms in horror at such developments? I suspect that they will, and yet the signs are there that not only players, but employers and players' families will refuse to tolerate the demands of the game. Edwards, Davies, J.P.R., Slattery and Dixon were missing in 1977 – why? Slattery again, Neary, Uttley, Leslie and Fenwick were missing from South Africa in 1980 – why? Terry Cobner, J.J. Williams, Roger Blyth, Paul Ringer, Derek Quinnell and myself all retired from the international scene while still playing for our respective clubs. Why? The game in the seventies made too many demands, and it is time for attitudes to be readjusted.

11

'Who Are You Playing On Saturday?'

Rugby may be changing its course in several ways. A certain amount of professionalism may creep in, with players being paid compensation wages for the time lost. Tours to foreign parts will inevitably become shorter and the amount of television coverage given to the game will force the authorities to put the image of rugby union right.

What we saw on the Twickenham field against England in 1980, in what inevitably will become known as the 'Ringer' match, was the culmination of several months of intense television and newspaper pressure. It was an unsavoury match with far too much needle. Some have suggested that it was an expression of nationalism by the Welsh, generated by the resentment of unemployment and economic depression in the valleys. Poppycock! Weeks before, when Wales had played France in another gruesome encounter, there had been yards of newspaper columns devoted to the decline of the Welsh dominance in the home championship. England had a good team on paper, and given that factor you could keep Fleet Street writing for a decade. It is true that there were cracks in the Welsh make-up before the 1979 championship – after all, they were still recovering from the loss of Gareth, J.P.R., Gerald and J.J. Naturally the Welsh team were written off by people who should have known better as non-starters. And so the Welsh players reacted with a certain amount of fire.

I don't condone what happened at Twickenham,

158

though I thought the Ringer incident the most trivial reason for sending a man off that I've ever seen. If that deserved a finger pointing to the dressing room then there are players in both England and Wales, and in every rugby-playing nation in the world, who would hardly emerge from the dressing room. But no matter; the press had done their job before the Twickenham match, had charged the Welsh players with grievous bodily harm in the preceding match against France, *and* found them guilty.

Yet the incident underlined a serious trend in first-class rugby. By definition rugby is a physical game, and mauls, rucks and tackles tax not only the physical resources of a player but also his tolerance. Tragically, players get hurt at the bottom of the pile-ups and mauls, but in the quest for ball possession the injuries and gashes are almost part and parcel of the game. The administrators have tried their best to rid the game of the accidental injury by restricting the amount of time allowed for a pile-up. This is obviously a commendable trend, but what I find far more sinister in rugby is the thug and criminal who enjoys maiming and hurting his opponents.

There are players in first-class rugby in Wales who think nothing of kicking an unprotected head in a maul. There are those who take immense pleasure in seeing an opponent squirm as a result of an illegal ploy. If the various committees of the leading first-class clubs don't know who these people are, then it is time for them to consult the players themselves. I have had a list of 'cloggers' and 'thugs' in my possession for some time. I hate playing against these men, since you know that they will attempt to get away with whatever they can when the referee isn't looking. The tragedy of it all is that a number of these players don't have to resort to question-able tactics at all. They have enough ability to reach the highest grade in representative football. Some of them have done so.

It may seem somewhat hypocritical of me to ask the

authorities to single out the guilty ones after being personally involved in one of the most controversial injuries in club rugby. At the time it was called the 'Ralston affair', a sequence of events that brought out the worst in some people, had the rugby officials of Richmond acting like KGB agents, and the press editors of both Welsh and English newspapers sending reporters to villages in West Wales that they couldn't even pronounce, let alone spell, accurately. Perhaps it is as well that I dwell on the Ralston affair, since it illustrates what can go wrong when rugby people hang out their washing for all to see.

Llanelli were involved in a normal fixture with Richmond; up until then, both clubs had got along famously well. The trip to London and staying in one of the 'carpeted, colour TV' hotels were always anticipated eagerly by the Llanelli lads. The games between the two clubs had always been fair, and I can't remember any previous violence between the two sides. In the seventies it was, I must be honest, a plum Saturday for us, since at that time we were a little too strong for Richmond; lest anybody accuse me of being arrogant, check the scores.

On this particular Saturday Llanelli were again on paper unlikely to lose to Richmond. It was a hard game, but nevertheless a fair one. Chris Ralston left the field with a head injury and after the game I was told that he'd been given eleven stitches. It sounded an awful lot of stitches at the time, but as the champagne flowed in the Richmond clubhouse afterwards, the incident and the injury were forgotten, and certainly there was no indication of any accusing finger.

The injury must have pricked my conscience somewhat, though; since I remember turning to Llanelli coach John Maclean during the train journey home to Wales and saying that I was concerned about what had happened to Chris, who'd been a Lion and a friend of mine in South Africa in 1974. If it had been done deliberately, I said, then the guilty person must be punished and told that he was no longer welcome at

Llanelli. At the time, I had a suspicion that the kick was a deliberate one, and I wanted no part of it. John agreed, and as the train sped along its way back to Llanelli, captain and coach were determined to find out what exactly had happened.

The next time the Llanelli team were due to meet was on the Monday evening for training. I was preparing to go out, collecting my togs, when suddenly on the network television news at six p.m. Chris Ralston's face appeared and the newsreader said, 'Chris Ralston says he was kicked deliberately by a Llanelli forward and is to seek legal advice.' My heart sank! Chris had run to the press! We hadn't been given a chance to find out who had been responsible. I appreciated even then what the repercussions of this story would be. My first reaction was to phone the Llanelli secretary Ken Jones, who confirmed that Richmond had sent a letter complaining about the injury that morning and had named two Llanelli players who they thought were involved. And this was the committee that two days earlier had been buying champagne for the Llanelli team.

On the way down to Stradey I mulled over in my mind what to do next. I had no doubt that the rest of the boys would have seen the broadcast or at least heard about it by now. The first person I saw at Stradey was Derek Quinnell, and we quickly sought a quiet corner in the club. Derek's attitude was direct and emphatic.

'I don't want to go down on balls against English clubs knowing that there might be a few vengeful forwards around.'

So we agreed that the culprit, if there was one, had to be found. When we gathered the forwards together, my initial fears were confirmed. They had all heard of the broadcast and all eight forwards who had been at Richmond denied any knowledge of the incident. I hadn't expected any other kind of reaction really, especially since the words 'legal action' were flying around like a tranquillizing opium. That night, the committee decided that it had no other alternative but to suspend all eight forwards.

Then there followed a vicious attack by the press on prop Charles Thomas. Though he had been named by Richmond in their letter, there was not one shred of evidence against him, and his fellow forwards maintained that Charlie hadn't been anywhere near the maul where Ralston claimed that he'd been kicked. Nevertheless the reporters turned up in their droves outside his home expecting to see some semi-human ogre feasting himself on a carnivorous diet of flesh and bones. As far as the press was concerned, and indeed some very erudite members of the Richmond club, Charlie was guilty of the offence and that was that. His trial in the tabloids lasted for weeks, and it must have been a trying time for him. Sensibly, however, he kept himself out of the argument. Two days after the Monday meeting, the entire Llanelli pack were dropped for our next game, against, of all people, Swansea. Yet there was still no response from the forwards as to who was responsible. The Llanelli committee were then left with two alternatives. Either to ask all eight players to leave the club, thus labelling them as liars, or to reinstate all eight, giving them the benefit of the doubt and concluding it had been an accident. They chose the latter option.

What irked me most about the affair was Chris Ralston's attitude. He had run to the press without even consulting the Llanelli players or committee. During the course of events, John Maclean, Derek and I travelled to the Severn Bridge to meet Chris to discuss the issue. At that meeting Chris apologized for running to the papers; by that time, though, it was too late, the damage had been done. Had he phoned on the Sunday after the game and explained his grievances, then I am sure that I, or somebody else in the club, would have investigated the incident and probably would have been successful in finding the culprit. Of one thing I am sure. Had I found out who was responsible, that player would never have played for Llanelli again. Either that or I would have left the club.

The repercussions of the Ralston affair were immediate and cruel. Llanelli travelled to Coventry shortly after the Swansea game and we were catcalled from the kick-off. There were shouts of 'animals' throughout the game. Perhaps the feelings of the Midland, and English, crowd were understandable; less so were the feelings of the Welsh crowd at Cardiff in a later game who were just as vitriolic in their contempt for the Llanelli club. Chris Ralston and the Richmond club had done Llanelli RFC no favours by accusing us in public and giving us no chance of settling the matter in the right, and most effective, way. I felt, as I feel now, angry with Chris and his club for the way in which they went about things. I want nothing to do with Richmond RFC ever again.

That may seem a petty and immature attitude to take. Time may well heal that wound, but I feel that somehow we must get back to the fundamental reason why thousands of people either turn up in their togs on a Saturday or watch from the terraces. It is a sport to be enjoyed, to be played in a sporting manner. That statement may seem a simpleton's observation. But I feel that too many pressures are being brought into the game and these have produced their inherent dangers. Rugby now shares prominence with soccer in the papers, and the private lives of schoolteachers, engineers and council workers who trot out for their rugby clubs on Saturdays have become fair game for the news reporter. Few of the amateur rugby-players are equipped to deal with such exposure. The seasoned international after receiving a few caps becomes accustomed to the constant questioning and knows that it is best to limit answers to vague ambiguities. Few pressmen bothered the elder statesmen because they know that the old foxes will never say anything controversial. But the newcomer to the Welsh team is always vulnerable.

I can recall Chris Lander of the *Mirror* landing me right in it. He'd phoned me up just before a Scotland international. 'How are you going to beat Scotland on Saturday?' he asked.

I thought the answer was ambiguous enough. 'Oh', I replied, 'I think if things go well, and we get the right sort of ball, and the conditions are good, we might run with it. But we'll see how it goes.' I must have given the same standard reply a hundred times. The next morning the headlines blazed: 'LOOK OUT SCOTLAND? BENNETT AIMS TO TAKE YOU ON!' I could have murdered Chris Lander on the spot. Here I was, going up to Scotland five feet seven inches in my stocking feet, threatening to take on single-handed the might of Scotland. I knew exactly what the Scottish team would make of such a headline. It would set them up ready and willing to stuff the words down my throat. So my advice to any youngster is to watch out since, though Chris and several others of that peculiar tribe called journalists are friends of mine, they have a job to do – and that is to get as much out of a quote or a story as they possibly can.

To be fair, apart from that little misinterpretation of words by Chris Lander and the run-in I had with John Reason in South Africa, I have been reasonably well treated by the media. The calls at all hours are sometimes annoying, but gradually it becomes part and parcel of the scene, and Pat knows only too well how to deal with them. I have gradually built up a list of those I trust and those I treat warily. The Welsh press, I suspect, recognize that there is little to be gained from sniping at individuals since the rugby community in South Wales is so close and parochial.

J.B.G. Thomas of the *Western Mail* and the now retired Viv Jenkins of the *Sunday Times* are two who have not only been kind to me personally, but also to many other players. Indeed, both have been called upon several times to act as troubleshooters when the temperature between press and player has tended to become a little warm. But the journalist sitting in an office in London, far removed from the familiarity of the South Wales rugby atmosphere, is a different animal altogether. There is little doubt in my mind that the pressure of bad press ultimately forced Paul Ringer to retire from international rugby. No matter what the rights or wrongs were of what happened at Twickenham in 1980, Paul served his sentence and should have been allowed to continue his career. He claimed that certain members of the London press had carried out a 'character assassination' campaign against him and felt justifiably aggrieved. Yet few people stop and wonder about the consequences of such snipes and insinuations as he was victim of. If the amateur player had the machinery to defend himself in public, then the balance would be somewhat fairer. Yet, the player who becomes involved in a public debate has so much to lose, and the authorities, I know, would be the last to defend even one of their own.

I remember having a long conversation with the New Zealand lock, Frank Oliver, when we were both invited out to South Africa for the Northern Transvaal anniversary games. The Welsh public were still feeling angry about the 'Andy Haden' incident in which, as well as engineering a penalty by falling out of a line-out, Haden also kept the New Zealand-Welsh fraternal relationship on a cold-war plane. Both Frank and I agreed that true genuine sportsmanship had gone out of the game. The *camaraderie* which had been there in the days of Whineray, Meads, Nathan and the Clarke brothers had somehow disappeared. It has been replaced by the dour attitude of Ian Kirkpatrick's All Blacks and the unhappy bunch of tourists called the '77 Lions. My contention is that the pressures on the modern player, who lives in an area populated by fanatics besotted by the desire and need to win, have to a large extent killed the enjoyment and the spontaneity of playing rugby.

We've become orthodox in our play and in our training. Coaches have become stereotyped, and it saddens me to know that the moves being practised on a Monday evening at Stradey or St Helen's are being worked upon at a hundred grounds in South Wales on the same night. The individual who can use his pace, and side-step to get out of trouble or follow his intuition for a counterattack is now a rare animal in Welsh rugby,

165

simply because the set play has been taught as either a safety-valve mechanism or a percentage move. Ironically is it always the unorthodox player that catches the eye. It is all too apparent that Wales will sorely miss the Geralds and Gareths of this world, or those players who possess the flair and the genius to ignore the coaching manual. Coaching didn't provide Gareth with the presence of mind to decide when to employ those metre-eating kicks of his, and no amount of coaching sessions could have taught Gerald his Fred Astaire routine on the Arms Park touch-lines. But it worries me to think that somewhere in the schools and on the playing fields of Wales there may be a youngster who is having the flair coached right out of his system. It is time to re-examine our attitude before the intuitive jinx and the side-step disappear.

The price of failure in Wales is high. No other nation that I have come across honours its rugby playing with so much diligent attention ... and no other crowd accepts its defeats so grudgingly. The bars at Stradey are empty after a Llanelli defeat, and the post-mortem after a Welsh defeat takes on the dimensions of those that followed the Wall Street crash. In my last season, I readily admit that I did have a hankering to have one last go in the international arena. I knew that Gareth Davies, the incumbent outside-half, was having injury problems and that if I informed the Welsh selectors of my availability there was a slight possibility that they might consider me for the Welsh squad. But apart from having too many enemies on or near the selection committee, I also knew that if I was selected and played badly the public, fickle as they are, would only remember me for that one game. It may seem again to be an arrogant or unkind remark, but I know only too well that the old saying, 'you are only as good as your last game' is particularly true in Wales. I know that I couldn't bear the pressure of having a bad game for Wales, because I had experienced the 'Coventry' stares and mumblings behind my back before.

After more than a decade of playing in Welsh rugby I have seen the atmosphere in the various changing rooms become far more intense. I look back with affection to those jokers who played in the centre for Llanelli, John 'Bach' and Gwyn Ashby – only national service orders would have got those two anywhere near a squad session; I tend to believe that the game is losing its characters. I hope that I'm proved wrong and that a new more adaptable type of player is emerging. What I have realized is that players as well as administrators have been overtaken by events. In many ways the reintroduction of the Schweppes WRU Cup is a welcome addition to the fixture lists. The actual day of the cup final has all the trappings of an international. In addition to the cup there are merit tables, pennant championships and the unofficial *Western Mail* championship. The organization of the cup on a knock-out basis is a healthy one, but how on earth the winners of these other competitions are worked out I'll never know. There is a desperate need in Wales for us to work out a simple and effective championship system, and one that is acceptable to all, sponsor included. When Llanelli first played in the cup final against Neath in 1972, there could only have been some 10,000 people at the Arms Park. Since then, the cup final, and even some of the semifinals are sell-out matches. It has prestige, and it is a lifesaver for the finances of any club, especially for some of the lesser clubs who might enjoy a good run in the competition. In the same context, an early exit from the competition for a larger club will produce a very sore-headed treasurer. Nevertheless, it has again brought pressure to bear on the player, who now not only has to contend with the international matches and the training sessions but, because of the Cup schedule, might have to play in a vital semifinal between Welsh matches. Again I would suggest that the scheduling of the competition should be revised, since cup semifinals are every bit as taxing as an international match.

It is no wonder then that sometimes a player cracks

under the strain of it all. Gareth in the Welsh dressing room in Ireland summed it all up when he said, 'That's it, I've had enough.' He realized that his competitive spirit just wasn't there, even though he still reckons he's good enough to play Welsh league football for Swansea City; but the outside influences gradually grind you to a halt.

My club rugby for Llanelli for two seasons out of the public eye has been enormously enjoyable; being called a veteran by the Stradey press scribes has its compensations – they don't expect an old man to perform well. Mind you, with J.J., Paul Ringer, Derek Quinnell, Roy Bergiers there too, the post offices on Tuesday could become quite busy with pension applications. It has been pleasant though to see some new names making the grade and, given time and responsible coaching, I think there are prosperous days ahead for the club. David Nicholas is already on his way at long last into the international record books and before long I'm sure that the likes of Mark Douglas, Martin Gravelle and Kevin Thomas will also press hard for recognition. I wonder at times, though, if the Llanelli committee deserves the talents of such young players.

This last season some of the most faithful of the servants have decided to hang up their boots. J.J. Williams, Gareth Jenkins, Roy Bergiers and Selwyn Williams have all decided to call it a day. These players are all household names to Welsh rugby supporters and the idols of many a schoolboy. Yet when at the beginning of this season, the Llanelli committee decided that it was time to prune the playing staff, instead of a public thank-you for all they had done for the club during a decade, they all received a note telling them that they were no longer in the Llanelli squad. It wasn't even a personal note: a few sentences copied on a Xerox machine informing the player that, because of the large number of hopefuls in the Llanelli squad, some of the old 'uns had to go. When I think of the undivided loyalty which people like Gareth Jenkins and Selwyn Williams gave to Llanelli, the hundreds of matches up and down the country, the injuries suffered and the entertainment provided ... I really think that the Llanelli committee must have had leave of their senses. Some of us had been fortunate to have been selected for Wales and Lions tours, so you could say that we have had the ultimate rewards of the game, but Jenkins and Williams, who should have received far more recognition, were left at the end of the day, with a note ... Thanks very much!

Such ungracious behaviour isn't limited to the Llanelli selector. This season if the Welsh selectors were determined to drop J.P.R. Williams and Steve Fenwick from the national team, why didn't they give these marvellous servants the chance of quietly announcing their desire to take a back seat. But then four of the five selectors had suffered the indignity of being dropped by Wales during their playing days, so what was good enough for them ...

I am not arguing in favour of monetary recognition, nor do I think that players should be fêted with garlands of roses. My only contention is that, after a decade of service to one club and its fortunes, be they bad or good, these players deserve something greater than a note saying, 'We would like to thank you for your services.' Unless such committee people wake up to their responsibilities, then they might find players beginning to question their loyalty to the club. One only has to look at the manner in which the Pontypridd committee has appreciated the contribution of that bionic nightmare of an opponent, Bob Penberthy, to find out why he's so devoted to the Pontypridd cause.

Even so I would never play for any other club. Despite all my criticisms, and they are, I hope, meant to be constructive ones, Llanelli RFC is still the greatest club in the world. After returning home from a long tour, and finding the garden immaculate and a number of odd jobs done around the house, you appreciate your friends and neighbours. I have friends in the Llanelli area who have stuck with me through thick and thin.

169

Whenever there's been something approaching a domestic crisis in the home, there are people that I can always turn to, who will willingly lend a hand. The members of the Liberal and Conservative clubs, Elvet Jones, the Llanelli chairman, Geoff the barber, John the bookie and honourable counsel John Lloyd, they have all been amazing friends. I've no doubt that I've taxed their patience on numerous occasions.

Even now, after being a bit *twp* (daft) after a reception in Cardiff and celebrating too much, I find people who are willing to drive me around on calls and messages. Felinfoel and Llanelli are indeed my life blood, and no one will ever know how much I owe the people for their kindness and generosity. For me, odd jobs around the house are tortuous expeditions into the unknown. Hammering nails into walls nearly always culminates in medical surgery. Fixing plugs into machines endangers the wiring at the local electricity substation. I've spent the last two Christmas Eves helping Santa Claus wrap his presents only to be told by Steven on Christmas morning that Father Christmas must have been very tired when he packed the presents since he'd messed it all up. It's no wonder that I appreciate friends who are good with hammers or handy with instruction leaflets. It's the same with the car: Pat will testify that, before now, I've left it on the side of the road with a flat tyre and hitch-hiked home rather than be confronted with the ordeal of changing it. Practicality deserted me at childbirth; hence I desperately need friends and relatives who can bail me out when Pat's tolerance has been expended. The people of Felinfoel and the townspeople of Llanelli have given us marvellous support. Without their encouragement I don't know whether I would have pursued my rugby career. They rallied round when we lost our first child, they were there when I was told that I'd never play rugby again, and they turned up in their thousands when I returned home from South Africa and New Zealand.

Those receptions were unbelieveable and humbling:

bunting, placards and smiling faces lining the streets of
Felinfoel, as the village people tried to express their
feeling that they were proud to have one of their own in
the limelight. Indeed, it was their celebration, since they
were as much a part of me as I was of them. It was
difficult to fight back the tears as one saw friends and
neighbours deck their homes with Union Jacks, Red
Dragons and 'Welcome home, Phil' signs. Old men who
had known me since childhood, and young faces that
were being told by their mothers what the fuss was all
about, turned up in their thousands ... and the reception
after the New Zealand tour was that much more welcome. Little do they know how much comfort I draw
from their support. It is summed up by a comment from
the captain of the Felinfoel cricket team who welcomed
me back from South Africa.

'Thank God you're back, 'cause it's been hell since
you've been out there. Every time the Lions went into an
attacking position, the umpires drew the stumps and we
all had to gather around a radio set.'

This devotional support for a game is as much a part
of the community as the Klondyke steelworks or the
Felinfoel brewery. I hope in some way to repay the
kindness shown over the years; yet it seems an impossible
task.

12

A Fitting End

I began my story at Stradey Park in 1972 when Llanelli faced the challenge of the touring All Blacks. I suppose it is fitting that I should end at the same ground with the same opponents eight years later. Wales, in centenary-celebrating mood, had invited the New Zealanders to play five matches in Wales.

It was the showpiece of the season. The games against the World and President's fifteens were glamorous affairs, but this was the game that counted for me – Llanelli against New Zealand. I had something to prove after the events of 1977 and, from the middle of the summer as I donned tracksuit and running shoes, I had one encounter in mind. This would be my last opportunity to meet the All Blacks.

First they played Cardiff, who had got off to an unsettled start to the season. Then it was our turn. The air was again full of expectation, with pundits and backroom bar boys arguing about whether Llanelli could repeat the historic triumph of 1972. Personally I didn't think that we stood much of a chance since the Llanelli forwards seemed a bit on the small side compared with our 1972 team. But there was no questioning the spirit of the Llanelli lads. The players met at the Ashburnham golf club, and we were again treated to one of those inspiring monologues from Carwyn James.

Our skipper from that memorable day in 1972, Delme Thomas, followed him with a talk about our commitment to Llanelli Rugby Club, which brought memories flooding back to the Llanelli changing room of eight years before. The coach John Maclean then set about giving us a detailed analysis of how the All Blacks could be beaten and reminding every player of his duties for the afternoon. John, his eyes nervously darting around the room, was nearly in a state of exhaustion some two hours before the kick-off.

I suppose I was wiser and more mature than I had been on that memorable occasion in 1972, but the nervousness eventually got through to me too.

By the time we reached Stradey Park the skipper Ray Gravell was so excited he was almost in a straitjacket state of excitement. Ray is one of the most emotional people that I've ever met. He's a born worrier, and if he's not concentrating on his rugby, he's busy solving the economic problems of Wales when his nationalistic revolution takes over. He simply couldn't keep still, humming Dafydd Iwan's latest song about Maggie Thatcher and asking us all if we liked it ... and if we didn't, why not? It was time for him to give his pre-match talk. I still don't know what he did to the English language that afternoon, but I'm told on good authority by Carwyn, who recorded it, that there were some unusable words in it. His parting shot before we went onto the field was a classic.

'Boys! ... Boys! [and the tears in his eyes spoke volumes] I've got a telegram here I want to read to you ... "Best wishes to my son" it says, boys. "All my love" ... and do you know who signed it? "Best wishes from Mam and Shamrock." *Chi'n gwbod pwy yw Shamrock bois? Y gath!* Do you know who Shamrock is, boys? the f— cat, the f — cat sent us a telegram!'

What else could we do but go out and play our best for Ray and his blessed cat. It was an exciting and hard game and we surprised a number at Stradey that afternoon with our tenacity to take the punishment and then spring back into life. The ill-feeling between the Welsh and the New Zealanders had been long forgotten, mainly due to the superb management and the captaincy of the previous All Blacks tour in 1979. Graham Mourie my old opponent was here again and leading an All Blacks team that had all the hallmarks of being one of the best touring sides of all times. Had they extended their tour I think we would have seen some great football from Graham's team. As it was, I think the Welsh supporters saw enough of them at the Arms Park, when they showed us how lethargic our rugby thinking had become in this country. But at Llanelli we gave them as good a game as they got, especially in the first half, and if things had gone a little better for us, then we could possibly have notched up a second victory over New Zealand. On the day, we lost to a better team who were only just finding their way as they prepared for the test match against Wales. Again though, the match will be remembered not for the quality of play, nor the fightback by the All Blacks in the second half. No; after the Deans, Meads and Haden incidents there was yet another to be added. This one will be remembered as the 'Hosie' incident, after the Scottish referee Alan Hosie.

In the dying minutes of the game there was a maul on the stand side of Stradey Park. The All Black lock Graeme Higginson on the blind side was seen by many to be raking one of the Llanelli players. There was an immediate uproar from the crowd and, though the play had been hard up until then, I hadn't seen anything like the ill-feeling that I had witnessed in New Zealand against the Lions. It had been a hard, gruelling match, but it hadn't been dirty; though Mr Hosie had asked both captains to cool their players a bit, I thought that that warning had been given as a precautionary measure rather than as a 'next one will be off' type of ultimatum. However, Alan Hosie strode over to Higginson and Graham Mourie and pointed the lock towards the changing room. I couldn't believe it. He was actually going to send an All Black off the field! I immediately ran over to the group and asked Mr Hosie – no, I pleaded with him – not to send the man off. All the good work done by the 1979 All Blacks could have been wiped out by that one little incident. The centenary year would be remembered for the 'Higginson' incident and all those futile accusations and counteraccusations would be inflamed once again. The noise from the crowd was unbearable and I didn't know whether they were in accord with Mr Hosie's decision or not. I didn't care. He simply had to be persuaded to change his mind. Somebody tugged on my shoulder and Ray Gravell now became involved. The incident hadn't been worthy of a sending off and, though I couldn't hear anything of what Mr Hosie was saying, I was determined that the name of Llanelli wouldn't be linked with another of those New Zealand incidents. The protestations must have had some effect since, without the penalty being taken the game ended with Alan Hosie pointing towards the changing room and asking both captains to accompany him to his quarters. Later he said that there had been no question of Higginson being sent off. I'll reserve judgement on that and let sleeping dogs lie.

In the morning press I was given a right roasting for becoming involved in the affair ... and for showing discourtesy to Alan Hosie's authority. The repercussions, it was written, would be enormous. We had been guilty of questioning the referee's judgement and of being instrumental in changing his mind. Our action was not in the spirit of the game. Balderdash! It was the spirit of the game that led Ray and me to interfere and not allow Graeme Higginson to become another press casualty.

It is the spirit of the game that is so lacking in today's rugby.

If I and others were wrong to get involved in that affair, let it be noted that I would do exactly the same again in similar circumstances. Whatever the knowledgable authorities declared in public, let them read a note sent to me from Grant Batty a few days after the Higginson event.

Dear Phil,

Just a note to say thanks for your attitude and action towards Graeme Higginson at the end of your match with the All Blacks. Your gesture has done a hell of a lot to restore sanity between New Zealand and Welsh rugby. I've written this before the Wales/All Blacks test match, but would wish that both teams play as well as they are capable of – regardless of the result.

BATTS